1992

Happy Birthday Betsy

nothing like good Irish food
& friends.

Affectionately, Claudia

Irish Cooking
Classic and Modern Recipes

Irish Cooking
Classic and Modern Recipes

ETHEL MINOGUE

CRESCENT BOOKS
NEW YORK

For Karim, Daragh, Shane and Peter,
and with thanks to
Sam, and Tim and Zoe Hill

A QUINTET BOOK

This 1989 edition published by Crescent Books,
distributed by Outlet Book Company, Inc.,
a Random House Company,
225 Park Avenue South,
New York, New York 10003

Reprinted 1991

ISBN 0-517-67378-9

8 7 6 5 4 3 2

This book was designed and produced by
Quintet Publishing Limited
6 Blundell Street
London N7 9BH

Creative Director: Peter Bridgewater
Art Director: Ian Hunt
Designer: Annie Moss
Editors: Beverly LeBlanc, Judith Simons, Susie Ward,
Henrietta Wilkinson
Home Economist: Ethel Minogue
Photographer: Tim Hill
Stylist: Zoe Hill
Ireland Photography: Trevor Wood, assisted by
Jonathan Higgins

Typeset in Great Britain by
Context Typesetting, Brighton
Manufactured in Hong Kong by
Regent Publishing Services Limited
Printed in Hong Kong

ADDITIONAL PICTURES
John Heseltine: page 52; Illustrated London New: pages
47 *b*, 87 *b*; Irish Tourist Board: pages 14 *t*, 38/9, 43 *t*;
Robert Opie Collection: pages 59 *r*, 99 *br*, Trevor Wood
and Michael Bull: pages 101 *b*, 115.

Contents

Introduction

TRADITIONAL IRISH FARE is famous for being simple and wholesome, and
based as it is on some of the finest ingredients to be found in the world
there is little need to dress it up with fancy sauces and dressings. Ireland
is a land of plenty: its seas and rivers team with fish and seafood, such as
salmon and trout, native oysters, lobsters, Dublin Bay prawns and giant
scallops: the unpolluted pastures produce the finest beef, lamb and pork
in the world; and the skies are full of game birds – pheasant, snipe,
partridges and wild duck are everyday fare for many country people.

Irish cooking has a long history, and some of its traditions, such as the
serving of boiled and roast meats on the same platter, date back to early
Celtic times when the land was governed by a legal system called the
Brehon Laws, which even laid down rules concerning food and
hospitality. However, in more recent times, the increasing dependence
of rural Ireland on the potato – a fickled crop at the best of times – com-
pounded by cruel economic and social policies, lead to the terrible
famines of the 1840s and '50s.

These tragedies virtually destroyed peasant cuisine. Dishes such as
pork ciste, spiced beef and soda bread pre-date the famine, but many
traditional dishes disappeared due to non-existent vegetable production.
The author remembers a time when it was impossible to buy anything
apart from potatoes, cabbage, carrots and onions in the west of Ireland
and only recently have more "exotic" foodstuffs like garlic, peppers, and
kiwi fruit become available.

The tradition of Irish cooking continued in the more prosperous
farmhouses and country estates, and this book is a collection of traditional recipes culled from old notebooks, Irish homes, hotels and
restaurants. The author is also indebted to Monica Sheridan and
Theodora Fitzgibbon, whose books and articles in *The Irish Times* have
inspired many Irish cooks. Many of the modern recipes are a result of the
author's experiments in a lighter style of cooking practiced in her own
restaurant. She has successfully dispelled the idea of Ireland as a culinary
desert and believes in using traditional wholesome ingredients so that
new dishes such as Sea Bass Wrapped in Seaweed, Cashel Cheese and
Celery Soup, Scallops in Champagne Sauce and delicious and unusual
salads are served along side traditional staples such as Brochan Roy,
oatcakes and Irish Stew.

A nation's diet is an important part of that country's history and
culture. Irish food is very close to the earth and this book provides the
best in both traditional and modern Irish cuisine to be heartily enjoyed
with good wine and convivial conversation.

Soups

LEFT
*Magnificent landscape, mountains
and lakes – the very stuff of the
countryside in the west of Ireland.
This is the heartland of Irish
traditional cooking, in which soups
play a prominent part.*

Mutton Broth with Barley

COOKING TIME: 1 HOUR 20 MINUTES

INGREDIENTS

1½ lb neck of lamb or mutton on the bone

2 large onions, chopped

¼ cup pearled barley

3 tbsp soaked haricot (white) beans

7½ cups brown broth (see Basic Recipes)

2 carrots, finely chopped

2 leeks, finely chopped

2 celery stalks, finely chopped

2 turnips, peeled and finely chopped

Salt and pepper

Chopped fresh parsley

▲ Trim any fat off the neck meat. If you are using the leg of mutton, ask your butcher to bone and roll it for you.

▲ Put the meat in a large pan. Add the chopped onions, the barley and beans. Simmer for 1 hour in the broth – skim, if necessary, and add all the vegetables. Continue to cook for about 20 minutes.

▲ Remove the bones before serving. Add salt and pepper to taste and garnish each bowl with chopped parsley.

Mutton broth used to be one of the staples in the Irish diet. Mutton is often difficult to get nowadays – the modern taste for young lamb has resulted in reduced quantities of mature meat. If you are serving Mutton in Caper Sauce as the main course, the leg of mutton may be cooked in this broth, which is then served as the first course. Otherwise neck of mutton is excellent for soup.

Brotchan Roy

COOKING TIME: 40 MINUTES

INGREDIENTS

5 cups chicken stock or milk (see Basic Recipes)

2 tbsp medium rolled oats

6 young leeks

2 tbsp butter

2 tbsp chopped fresh parsley

Salt and pepper

Pinch of ground mace

Cream and snipped chives, to garnish

▲ Bring the chicken broth or milk to a boil. Sprinkle in the oats, stirring all the time to prevent lumps.

▲ Cut the leeks – both white and green parts – into ½-in pieces. Wash them well and soften in the butter. Add the leeks to the simmering oat mixture.

▲ Cook for about 15 minutes. Add the snipped parsley, salt, pepper and mace.

▲ Serve in warm bowls, with a swirl of cream and snipped chives. Hot buttered oatcakes (*see* Oatcakes) are delicious with this soup.

OPPOSITE *The Irish are a race of farmers. County Donegal is famous sheep country and the mutton and lamb produced there is a basis for many soups and broths.*

Pea and Ham Soup

COOKING TIME: 2 HOURS OR MORE

▲ Soften the onions in the bacon fat. Put them in a large pan with the ham bone and add the drained peas, the bunch of herbs and bay leaf. Cover these with the broth or ham water. Bring the broth slowly to a boil, then simmer for 2 hours.

▲ Take out the bones – dice any ham or bacon trimmings, which can go back into the soup.

▲ If the soup is too thick, water or milk may be added to thin it. If you add milk, bring the soup to simmering point, but do not boil it.

▲ Season and serve with chopped mint and parsley. Small pieces of bacon are a nice addition.

INGREDIENTS

2 large onions

2 tbsp bacon fat

1 ham bone and trimmings

1 lb dried peas, soaked for at least 3 hours

1 bunch of fresh herbs

1 bay leaf

3¾-5 pt bacon broth or water used for boiling ham

Salt and pepper

Chopped fresh mint and parsley

*D*ried peas are a very popular vegetable in rural Ireland – until recently, except in the larger towns, it was almost impossible to buy any fresh vegetables apart from potatoes, onions, cabbage and carrots.

I felt quite shocked last year being able to buy peppers and kiwi fruit in a small village in West Clare.

Dried whole peas, marrow fats or split green peas may be used for this soup. Yellow peas may also be used and taste just as good, but the green color is more appealing with the ham.

White Onion Soup

COOKING TIME: 1 HOUR

This soup is a nice change from the French brown onion version. This is Theodora Fitzgibbons' recipe; like her, I remember onion soup being a cure-all in the same league as hot whiskey.

INGREDIENTS

¼ cup butter

1 lb onions, thinly sliced

2 cloves

2 heaped tbsp all purpose flour

Pinch of ground mace or grated nutmeg

1 bay leaf

4 cups chicken or pork broth
(see *Basic Recipes*)

1¼ cups milk

Salt and pepper

⅔ cup cream, or 1-3 tbsp grated
hard cheese

▲ Heat the butter and, when foaming, add the onions and the cloves. Let the onions soften, but not change color.

▲ Sprinkle over the flour. Mix well and cook, stirring constantly for 1 minute, then add the mace or nutmeg, the bay leaf and the broth. Stir all the time, until it boils and you can see that it is smooth.

▲ Simmer until the onions are well cooked, then gradually add the milk. Stir continuously and, when it boils, remove the cloves and bay leaf.

▲ This soup may be puréed, but is much nicer served as is with the addition of the cream or grated cheese.

IRISH STORES

Links between town and country have always been finely balanced in Ireland. Many of the stores are full of native products and many of the Irish still prefer the traditional cooking of their ancestors to modern convenience food.

IRISH COOKING

ABOVE LEFT *The imposing Rock of Cashel, crowned by its 13th-century cathedral, dominates this part of County Tipperary. The local cheese is equally celebrated.*

Sorrel Soup

COOKING TIME: 30 MINUTES

▲ Melt the butter. Chop the onion and the garlic and soften them in the butter. Wash and tear the sorrel, and melt it in the butter and onions. Add the broth and bring to a boil.

▲ Scatter in the oats and stir until cooked. Season the soup to taste and simmer for about an hour.

▲ Serve in warm bowls with a dollop of whipped cream.

INGREDIENTS

¼ cup butter

1 large Spanish onion

4 garlic cloves

1 lb sorrel

2½ quarts chicken broth
(see Basic Recipes)

2 tbsp medium rolled oats

Salt and pepper

⅔ cup heavy cream, lightly whipped

Cashel Cheese and Celery Soup

COOKING TIME: 45 MINUTES

▲ Soften the onions and celery in the butter. Add the cloves of garlic and the broth and simmer for about 40 minutes – or until the onions and celery are cooked.

▲ Blend the blue cheese and cream together and stir into the soup just before serving. Season to taste and serve in large warm bowls with croutons.

INGREDIENTS

3 large onions, sliced

1 head of celery, chopped

¼ cup butter

2 garlic cloves

5-7½ cups chicken or vegetable broth
(see Basic Recipes)

¼ lb Cashel blue cheese (other cow's
blue cheese will do)

A little cream to blend with the cheese

Cubes of bread fried in olive oil or
bacon fat and drained (croutons)

Leek and Mussel Soup

C O O K I N G   T I M E :   4 0 - 5 0   M I N U T E S

INGREDIENTS

5 pt mussels
4 leeks
2 shallots
2 garlic cloves
3 tbsp chopped fresh parsley
1 tbsp chopped fresh dill
1 tbsp snipped chives
½ bottle dry white wine
½ cup butter, cut into small cubes
5 cups fish broth (see Basic Recipes)
Small pinch of saffron soaked in water
Black pepper

▲ Prepare the mussels by removing the beards and any barnacles. Scrub well and rinse in clean water. Throw away any mussels that remain open when tapped – any mussels that feel very heavy will be full of mud and must be discarded as well.

▲ Chop the leeks, shallots and garlic finely. Put in a long pan with the mussels, parsley, dill and chives. Add the wine and place the pan on a high heat until the mussels are steamed open. Discard any mussels that remain firmly closed.

▲ Take out the mussels, shell and put aside. Reserve all the delicious liquid in the pan.

▲ Beat the butter cubes into the liquid and add the fish broth to the pan. Stir in the soaked saffron strands, simmer gently over a low heat for a few minutes and season with black pepper.

▲ Add the shelled mussels and heat in the liquid but do not boil, as the mussels will get leathery.

▲ Serve the soup in warm bowls garnished with more snipped chives and parsley. Pass slices of soda bread (*see* Brown Soda Bread).

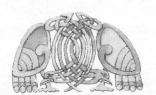

Fish Soup

COOKING TIME: 30 MINUTES

INGREDIENTS

*1-1½ lb mixed vegetables, finely
chopped (carrots, shallots, onions,
fennel, leeks, celery, tomatoes, potatoes)*
¼ cup butter
5 cups fish broth (see Basic Recipes)
Bay leaf and fresh herbs
2 garlic cloves
1½-2 lb firm white fish
1 glass dry white wine
2 tbsp chopped fresh parsley
⅔ cup light cream
Salt, pepper and paprika

▲ Toss the vegetables in 2 tbsp butter. Add the broth, herbs and garlic, and simmer until the vegetables are cooked.

▲ Cut the fish into chunks and poach gently in the wine. Remove the fish from the liquid, beat in the remaining butter and add to the broth and vegetables. Sprinkle in the chopped parsley, flake the fish, discarding the skin and bones, and add to the soup.

▲ Just before serving, add the cream and heat to just below boiling point. Do not boil. Season, and add a pinch of paprika in the bowls.

▲ This fish soup is very good served with croutons and garlic mayonnaise, and may also be made with either smoked cod or haddock. For another variation, add a pinch of curry powder instead of the paprika at the end.

Leek and Potato Soup

COOKING TIME: 50-60 MINUTES

1 lb leeks

1 lb floury potatoes

2 tbsp butter

*5 cups chicken or ham broth
(see Basic Recipes)*

*Large bunch of herbs, including some
celery tops*

Salt and pepper

*Cubes of bread fried in olive oil or
bacon fat and drained (croutons)*

Cream

▲ Slit the leeks lengthways, wash thoroughly and slice; peel and chop the potatoes. Melt the butter and soften the leeks in a pan. Add the potatoes and cook gently (do not fry) for about 10 minutes. Add the broth and bunch of herbs.

▲ Season to taste and simmer for about 1 hour.

▲ Add the fried croutons to the soup with a little cream when serving.

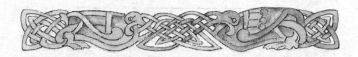

Appetizers
and Egg Dishes

Wild Mushroom Omelet   22

Wicklow Pancakes   23

Soft-Cooked Eggs in Ramekins with
Onion Sauce   24

Chicken Livers with Marsala   24

Black Pudding with Apple Purée   26

Fish Creams   27

Smoked-Salmon-Stuffed Tomatoes   28

Scrambled Eggs with
Smoked Salmon   29

Sweetbreads with Bacon   30

Buttermilk Crêpes   30

Chicken, Apple and
Blackpudding Filling   30

Spinach and Chopped
Egg Filling   31

LEFT
*A typical Connemara landscape,
with mountains sheltering rich
fields. In the Irish countryside, you
will find all sorts of foods growing
in the wild, many of which are used
in traditional Irish appetizers.*

Any edible wild mushrooms may be used for this. But be very careful if you are a novice mushroom hunter. Delicious as this is, you do not want to make it your last meal on earth.

INGREDIENTS

6 fresh eggs

1 tbsp chopped fresh herbs

Salt and pepper

1 lb chanterelle mushrooms

3 tbsp olive oil

Wild Mushroom Omelet

COOKING TIME: 10 MINUTES

▲ Beat the eggs with the herbs and salt and pepper. Slice the chanterelles.

▲ Put the olive oil in a non-stick skillet or pan. Cook the chanterelles for about 5 minutes, then add the egg mixture. Cook over a moderate heat until almost set. Fold and serve immediately.

RIGHT *Powerscourt, County Wicklow. Ireland has a country-house cooking tradition dating back to the days of the British Ascendancy, which has deeply influenced culinary style.*

Wicklow Pancakes

PREPARATION AND COOKING TIME:
10-15 MINUTES + 30 MINUTES

INGREDIENTS

1 lb onions

1½ lb potatoes

6 tbsp olive oil

Salt and black pepper

6 eggs

Chopped fresh parsley

▲ Peel and slice the onions and potatoes and stew in the olive oil until they are very well cooked – do try not to brown either the onions or the potatoes. Drain off the excess oil and season to taste.

▲ Beat the eggs in a large bowl, then add the potato and onion mixture, along with some chopped parsley. Put a little oil in a pan and pour some of the mixture in until it is nearly 1 in thick.

▲ Cook over a medium heat until reasonably firm, then turn over with the help of a dinner plate. Cook for a few minutes on the other side.

▲ Serve on a clean plate, cut into wedges, and eat hot or cold.

Chicken Livers with Marsala

Soft-Cooked Eggs in Ramekins with Onion Sauce

COOKING TIME: 25 MINUTES

INGREDIENTS

2 soft-cooked eggs per person
3 large Spanish onions
¼ cup butter or olive oil
A little cream or béchamel sauce

▲ Put the eggs in boiling water for exactly 4 minutes, then plunge them into cold water. When they are cool enough to handle, tap them all over with a spoon – don't bash them too hard or you will have a handful of soft-cooked egg. Peel the eggs carefully and place 2 per person in each ramekin.

▲ Thinly slice the onions and cook slowly in the butter or olive oil for at least 20 minutes. The onions must be very well-cooked, but not too brown. They may then be mixed with a little cream or béchamel sauce (*see* Basic Recipes).

▲ Put a few spoonfuls of the creamy onions on top of the eggs and warm the ramekins in the oven for 5 minutes. Finish under a broiler, until the sauce bubbles.

▲ There are delicious ways of varying this using tomato sauce, cheese sauce (*see* Basic Recipes) or sorrel sauce (*see* Poached Salmon with Sorrel Sauce).

Chicken Livers with Marsala

COOKING TIME: ABOUT 10 MINUTES

INGREDIENTS

¼ cup butter
½ Spanish onion, finely chopped
3 large garlic cloves
1 lb fresh chicken livers, cleaned and trimmed
Chopped herbs
1 glass Marsala
4 hard-cooked egg yolks, finely chopped or pressed through a strainer
Whole-wheat toast, buttered

▲ Melt the butter in a heavy-bottomed saucepan. Soften the onion and garlic in it. Add the trimmed livers and sauté until they are lightly cooked. Add the chopped herbs and cook for another few minutes.

▲ Pour in the Marsala and turn up the heat for about 2 minutes. Scrape into a bowl and chop roughly. Add the finely chopped or sieved egg yolks and pile onto triangles of buttered toast to serve. This dish is delicious hot or cold.

Soft-Cooked Eggs in Ramekins with Onion Sauce

RIGHT *Life in the country cottage revolves around its kitchen, where the entire household gathers to prepare and enjoy meals.*

Black Pudding with Apple Purée

COOKING TIME: 5 HOURS

INGREDIENTS

½ lb pig's liver
1½ lb chopped, unrendered lard
15 cups pig's blood
1 lb fresh bread crumbs
2½ cups water from cooking the liver
1 cup medium rolled oats
1 onion, chopped
½ tsp ground allspice
1 tsp each dried sage and thyme
Salt and pepper to taste

▲ Gently poach the liver in boiling salted water. Drain and reserve the water. Roughly chop the liver into a large bowl. Add the lard and all the other ingredients and stir very well.
▲ Pack the mixture into oiled heatproof bowls. Cover with wax paper and foil. Tie securely and steam for 4-5 hours. Unmold and leave until cold.
▲ Cut into slices and fry in bacon fat or lard, until crisp on both sides. Serve with broiled tomatoes and apple purée.

Apple Purée

COOKING TIME: 20 MINUTES

INGREDIENTS

2 lb tart cooking apples
1 tbsp light brown sugar
Chopped fresh sage

▲ Peel and core the apples. Stew with the brown sugar until soft.
▲ Mash with a fork and add a touch of chopped sage. Serve hot with the black pudding, pork chops or roast pork.

Fish Creams

INGREDIENTS

1 lb Finnan haddie

2 cups fresh bread crumbs

Salt and pepper

½ cup unsalted butter, melted

2 eggs, beaten

*2½ cups béchamel sauce
(see Basic Recipes)*

2 tbsp chopped fresh parsley

Grated nutmeg

▲ Lightly poach the Finnan haddie. Remove the skin and bones, then flake and mash the fish. Add the bread crumbs and seasoning. Mix in the melted butter and beaten eggs. Pour into a heatproof bowl or 4-6 ramekins.

▲ Cover with wax paper or foil, and steam over boiling water for 1 hour – less if you use the ramekins.

▲ Meanwhile, make a béchamel sauce and stir in the chopped parsley and grated nutmeg to taste.

▲ When the fish creams are cooked, unmold into a warmed serving dish and pour the sauce over them. Serve hot.

▲ Note: Vary the sauce by using cheese, cooked onions or mushrooms instead of the parsley.

COOKING TIME: 20 MINUTES

INGREDIENTS

8 medium-sized tomatoes

2 shallots

1 Spanish onion

½ lb smoked salmon

Bunch of fresh dill

2 cups fresh bread crumbs

1 lemon

1 tbsp light cream

1 tot pepper sauce

Bunch of watercress, to serve

OVEN TEMPERATURE: 350°F

▲ Preheat the oven. Cut the tops off the tomatoes. Scoop out the insides, throw away the centers and seeds and place the tomato pulp in a bowl. Chop the shallots and the onion finely and mix with the tomato pulp.

▲ Purée the smoked salmon and add to the bowl. Chop the dill finely, place in the bowl with the smoked salmon and all the remaining ingredients. Mix well.

▲ Spoon the mixture back into the tomatoes, put the tomato lids on and bake for about 20 minutes.

▲ Serve on a bed of watercress. These stuffed tomatoes are good hot or cold.

Scrambled Eggs with Smoked Salmon

COOKING TIME: 15 MINUTES

2 eggs per person

1 tbsp milk per person

Knob of butter

1 slice smoked salmon per person (or some trimmings), chopped

1 slice buttered whole-wheat toast per person

Chopped fresh dill or parsley

Black pepper

Lemon wedges

▲ Beat the eggs and milk until well blended but not frothy.

▲ Melt the butter over a low heat, add the eggs and milk and cook gently, adding the chopped salmon just before the eggs are ready. (Scrambled eggs should always be taken off the heat while the eggs are still very moist as they will continue to cook in their own heat.)

▲ Pile the egg and salmon mixture on the hot buttered whole-wheat toast, garnish with chopped dill or parsley, season with freshly ground pepper and top with a lemon wedge.

IRISH COOKING

Buttermilk Crêpes

INGREDIENTS
Heaped ¾ cup whole-wheat flour
Pinch of salt
1 egg
⅔ cup buttermilk
2 tbsp butter

▲ Mix the flour and salt; make a well in the middle. Stir in the egg and buttermilk, but do not beat too much at this stage. Melt the butter and beat into the mixture with a wooden spoon. Let stand for at least half an hour before using.
▲ Place a small ladle of batter on a crêpe pan, and shake the pan so the batter spreads evenly. When little holes appear on the pancake, it is ready to turn over. Do so.
▲ These pancakes are very light and may be kept warm in the oven until needed.
▲ Keep warm between 2 plates until they are ready to be filled.

Sweetbreads with Bacon
PREPARATION TIME: 3 HOURS

INGREDIENTS
2 lb sweetbreads, skinned and trimmed
1 egg, beaten
A little all purpose flour
¼ cup butter
2 garlic cloves
¼ lb button mushrooms
6 oz bacon slices, cut into 1-inch pieces
1 tbsp Madeira or sweet sherry
1 tbsp light cream
Chopped fresh parsley and snipped chives
Black pepper

▲ Soak the sweetbreads in cold, salted water for at least 3 hours. Blanch in fresh boiling water for 5-6 minutes. Drain and plunge into cold water. Cut off the gristly bits and the skin.
▲ Dip the sweetbreads in beaten egg and flour. Fry in butter for a few minutes and keep warm.
▲ Sauté the garlic, mushrooms and bacon in the butter. Stir in the Madeira and cream. Bubble for a few minutes. Add the sweetbreads, parsley and chives and some black pepper.
▲ Serve on toast or fried bread as an hors d'oeuvre, or with rice.

Chicken, Apple and Black Pudding Filling
COOKING TIME: 15-20 MINUTES

INGREDIENTS
4 shallots
2 dessert apples
1 large tart cooking apple
2 tbsp butter
6 oz black pudding
6 oz cooked chicken (a good way to use up leftover chicken)

▲ Chop the shallots, and peel and chop the apples, then cook in the butter until the cooking apple is mushy.
▲ Peel and cube the black pudding and chop the chicken. Add both to the apple sauce.
▲ Heat through, and fill the pancakes.

OPPOSITE *The south of Ireland's Catholic tradition is an integral part of the Irish heritage. This, too, has influenced Irish cookery, with the ritual of feast and fast days.*

Spinach and Chopped Egg Filling

COOKING TIME: 30 MINUTES

▲ Chop the onion and soften in the butter. Add the spinach and cook until soft and reduced to half its bulk.

▲ When the spinach is tender, add the béchamel sauce.

▲ Fold in the chopped hard-cooked egg, parsley, dill and grated nutmeg.

▲ Note: Buttermilk pancakes are also very good with scrambled eggs and smoked salmon as a filling (*see* recipe of that name). Also try cooked ham with onion in parsley sauce (*see* Béchamel Sauce in Basic Recipes).

INGREDIENTS

1 onion

2 tbsp butter

1 lb spinach, washed and stalks removed

1¼ cups béchamel sauce (see *Basic Recipes*)

4 hard-cooked eggs, chopped

Chopped fresh parsley and dill

Grated nutmeg

31

Fish and Shellfish

LEFT
*Towering cliffs dominate this
seascape near Portrush, in the north.
Fishing is one of Ireland's key
industries and the foods that come
from the sea are culinary staples.*

Fried Salmon Steaks with Herb Butter
COOKING TIME: 8 MINUTES

INGREDIENTS

4 fresh salmon steaks, about 6 oz each

½ cup butter

1 tbsp chopped fresh parsley

1 tbsp tarragon and fresh chives, chopped

▲ Lightly oil a griddle or large skillet. Place a salmon steak on the hot griddle and cook for about 4 minutes on each side.

▲ Work the butter, parsley and tarragon and chives together until you have a herb butter. Serve on hot plates with knobs of butter on top of the steaks.

▲ Salmon steaks make a quick-and-delicious meal served with minted new potatoes and green beans.

NOTE ON HERB BUTTERS: When fresh herbs are in season, it is a good idea to have a session of making different varieties. Herb and garlic butters may be kept in a roll shape in foil and frozen until needed. Soften unsalted butter and work in the chopped herbs:

Dill, parsley, lemon and tarragon butters are good with fish.

Tarragon, garlic and basil butter are delicious with chicken.

Thyme and rosemary butters are particularly good with lamb.

ABOVE LEFT *The rivers and lakes of the west are an ideal home for the princely salmon – hard to catch, but delicious to eat.*

Baked Stuffed Salmon with Cucumber Sauce

COOKING TIME: 1 HOUR

1 salmon, about 4 lb in weight
3 cups fresh bread crumbs
1 tbsp chopped fresh parsley
Grated zest of 1 lemon
⅓ cup mushrooms, finely chopped
2 hard-cooked eggs, chopped
Butter, melted
⅔ cup dry white wine

FOR THE CUCUMBER SAUCE:

1 cucumber, peeled, seeded
and chopped
1¼ cups liquid from cooking the fish
¼ cup unsalted butter, cut into cubes
OVEN TEMPERATURE: 350°F

▲ Preheat the oven. Clean and descale the salmon. Make the stuffing by mixing all the other ingredients except the wine in a bowl. Then put the stuffing inside the fish.

▲ Place the fish in a buttered baking dish. Pour the wine over and cover with foil. Bake for 15 minutes to the 1 lb. Baste occasionally.

▲ When cooked, remove the skin and small side bones and fins – keep hot.

▲ To make the sauce, cook the cucumber in the liquid from the baking dish over a high heat, then beat in the butter cubes gradually. When the sauce has thickened, pour over the salmon. Serve at once.

Poached Salmon with Sorrel Sauce

COOKING TIME: 8-10 MINUTES

*Allow 1 cutlet of salmon
(wild preferably) per person*

FOR THE SORREL SAUCE:

½ cup unsalted butter

*1 large bunch fresh sorrel, washed
and chopped*

1¼ cups heavy cream or crème fraîche

Salt and pepper

▲ Poach the salmon in boiling salted water for about 8 minutes. Remove and keep on a warm plate.

▲ Melt the butter in a saucepan. Add the chopped sorrel – it melts into the butter very quickly. When it has bubbled for a few minutes, add the cream and seasoning, bring to a boil and simmer for 10 minutes. If you are using crème fraîche, boil very rapidly for a few minutes.

▲ Pour the sauce over the poached salmon and serve immediately.

Baked Stuffed Trout

COOKING TIME: ABOUT 20 MINUTES

INGREDIENTS

4 one-portion-sized trout

1 cup fresh white bread crumbs

1 onion, finely chopped

Knob of butter

2 hard-cooked eggs, finely chopped

Grated lemon zest

4 small mushrooms, chopped

Hot-pepper sauce

Chopped fresh parsley

Salt and pepper

A little milk

White or red wine

OVEN TEMPERATURE: 350°F

▲ Preheat the oven. Clean the trout and pat them dry inside and out. Keep them in a cold place while you make the stuffing.

▲ Put the fresh bread crumbs in a bowl. Soften the onion in a little butter over a low heat and add to the bread crumbs, together with the lemon zest, finely chopped hard-cooked eggs, chopped mushrooms, hot-pepper sauce, parsley and seasoning to taste. Moisten with a little milk until the stuffing holds together.

▲ Stuff each trout with the mixture. Splash with a little wine and then wrap in foil or wax paper. Cook in a medium oven for about 20 minutes, or until the fish feels firm.

▲ Serve with parsley sauce (*see* Basic Recipes).

ABOVE *Trout, too, team in Irish rivers and the cooking method described here is ideally suited to preserving the fresh flavor of the fish.*

Scallops in Champagne Sauce

COOKING TIME: 15 MINUTES

INGREDIENTS

8 large scallops on the shell, if possible
4 scallions
Peeled fresh ginger root, to taste
2 garlic cloves
1/4 cup butter, melted
1 glass Champagne
Chopped fresh Italian parsley

▲ Remove the scallops from the shell using a short bladed knife. Discard the black bits and keep the white flesh and the coral. Keep any liquid from the shell and reserve the shells.

▲ Slice the scallions, ginger and garlic. Fry for a few minutes in the melted butter, then add the sliced scallops and their liquid. Toss the shellfish and onion mixture over a high heat for about 5 minutes. Remove the large pieces from the pan with a slotted spoon and keep warm.

▲ Pour the glass of Champagne into the juices in the pan. Cook on a high heat until the sauce is reduced. Serve the chopped scallops on the deep half shell with the sauce. Garnish with the chopped parsley.

This may sound rather extravagant, but it requires very little Champagne. It is also no hardship to drink the rest of the bottle while eating the scallops!

RIGHT *Ireland's scallop beds are justly famous and scallops fresh from the sea can be bought in many coastal-town markets, such as Ballybunion.*

Scallops on the Shell with Mushrooms and Duchesse Potatoes

COOKING TIME: 30-40 MINUTES

▲ Wash and clean the scallops. Poach for 5 minutes on top of the stove in a court bouillon made with 1¼ cups water and the wine, herbs, onion, salt and pepper.

▲ Drain the scallops, reserving the court bouillon, and slice them. Slice the mushrooms. Melt about ¼ cup butter in a pan and toss the mushrooms and scallops in it for a few minutes. Keep warm in a covered dish.

▲ In a saucepan, melt ½ cup butter and add the flour. Make a roux and cook for a few minutes. Cool the roux a little, then strain the reserved court bouillon and add to the roux very gradually. Stir with a whisk to prevent lumps. Bring to a boil, stirring with the whisk, and boil for 2 minutes.

▲ Take the sauce off the heat and thicken with two egg yolks, beaten with some of the court bouillon. Heat to simmering point, but do not boil, or the eggs will cook and go lumpy. Whisk ¼ cup butter into the sauce and season to taste.

▲ Preheat the oven. Clean the scallop shells. Put a spoonful of sauce on each shell. Top with the scallops and mushrooms with 2 bits of coral on each shell. Cover with more sauce and scatter bread crumbs on top.

▲ Pipe some mashed potato around the edge of the shell and brown in a very hot oven. Serve immediately.

INGREDIENTS

12 scallops and 6 shells
1 glass dry white wine
Bunch of sweet fresh herbs
Bay leaves
1 onion, sliced
Salt and freshly ground white pepper
1½ cups button mushrooms
1 cup unsalted butter
1 tbsp all purpose flour
2 egg yolks
Fresh bread crumbs
4 cups well-flavored mashed potatoes

OVEN TEMPERATURE: 350°F

Mussel and Onion Stew

COOKING TIME: 80 MINUTES

5 pt mussels

⅔ cup dry white wine and water, mixed

6 Spanish onions, sliced

¼ cup butter or olive oil

4 shallots, chopped

6 garlic cloves

2 carrots, chopped

4 potatoes

*Fresh parsley, thyme and bay leaf
tied together*

Chopped fresh parsley

Black pepper

▲ Scrub and debeard the mussels. Discard any that remain open when tapped. Place them in a large saucepan with the white wine and water. Cook on a high heat until the mussels are open – remember to discard any that remain firmly shut. Remove the mussels and strain the liquid and reserve.

▲ In another pan, soften the onions in butter or olive oil. Add the shallots, garlic and chopped carrots. Peel and slice the potatoes, put them in the pan with the herbs, parsley and the cooking liquid from the mussels. Season to taste with pepper. Simmer for about 1 hour.

▲ Meanwhile, shell the mussels, if wished, and reserve.

▲ Take a ladle full of the vegetable broth from the pot, making sure you include some potatoes, and purée. Add to the rest of the vegetables again and put all the mussels into the pot. Simmer until the mussels are hot.

▲ Serve in deep bowls with wedges of garlic bread.

Stuffed Mussels

COOKING TIME: 20 MINUTES

INGREDIENTS

48 large mussels
White wine
1 cup unsalted butter
10 garlic cloves, crushed
2 cups bread crumbs
Lemon wedges

▲ Debeard and scrub the mussels. Throw away any mussels that remain open when tapped. Steam open the mussels in a little white wine and water. Discard any that remain closed. Drain and take off the top shell.

▲ Soften the butter a little with your hands. Add the crushed garlic cloves and work the bread crumbs into the garlic butter.

▲ Put a knob of the stuffing on each mussel and place under a hot broiler.

▲ Serve very hot with lemon wedges and crusty French bread.

Oysters in Champagne Sauce

Fried Oysters

COOKING TIME: 10 MINUTES

INGREDIENTS

20 oysters

FOR THE BATTER:

Heaped ¾ cup all purpose flour

Salt and pepper

Pinch of cayenne pepper

1 egg

⅔ cup milk

Oil for frying

Lemon wedges

▲ Mix the dry ingredients in a bowl. Make a well in the center and mix in the egg and the milk, making a smooth batter. Leave for 30 minutes.

▲ Open the oysters, dip them in the batter and fry in hot oil. Drain on kitchen towels. Serve hot with lemon wedges.

Oysters in Champagne Sauce

COOKING TIME: 20 MINUTES

INGREDIENTS

⅔ cup Hollandaise sauce
(see Basic Recipes)

2 shallots, finely chopped

1 glass Champagne

16 oysters on-the-half-shell

▲ Make the Hollandaise sauce (*see* Basic Recipes). Add some finely chopped shallots and the glass of Champagne to the sauce.

▲ Spoon a little of the sauce on each oyster, bubble under the broiler for less than 2 minutes and serve.

ABOVE *Fresh oysters from Ireland's coasts, such as those from Tralee Bay in County Kerry, can simply be eaten raw, with a touch of lemon and accompanied by Ireland's equally celebrated beer – Guinness.*

*T*he best oysters in Ireland come from Galway, where every September there is a great oyster festival. It is really a sacrilege to cook such oysters. They are best eaten on the half shell, served on a bed of crushed ice and seaweed, with a lemon wedge and fresh whole-wheat bread and butter.

Recently, the Portuguese type, or rock oysters, have been cultivated on the northwest coast of Ireland. They do not have a "season," like the Galway oysters, and do not have such a sweet taste. When they are very fresh, however, they really taste of the sea. They tend to be cheaper than the natives, so it is more feasible to use them for cooking.

In the United States, there is yet another variety with a rough shell like the Portuguese oyster.

Angels on Horseback
COOKING TIME: 10 MINUTES

INGREDIENTS

12 oysters
12 bacon slices
12 wooden toothpicks
12 triangles of fried bread

▲ Open the oysters and take out the flesh. Roll 1 bacon slice around each oyster. Secure with a toothpick.
▲ Cook under a hot broiler and serve on hot triangles of fried bread.

ABOVE *Wherever you go on the Irish coast, you will find fishermen, fishing boats, the opportunity to try your skills at sea fishing and the reward of eating your catch.*

Fish Steaks with Mussels

Cod Baked with Bacon
COOKING TIME: 65 MINUTES

INGREDIENTS
1 Spanish onion, sliced

6 tbsp butter

1 lb potatoes, parboiled and thinly sliced

Salt and pepper

4 good-sized cod steaks, or firm white fish steaks of your choice

½ lb smoked bacon

1¼ cups light cream or milk

Chopped fresh parsley

OVEN TEMPERATURE: 350°F

Cod Baked with Bacon

▲ Preheat the oven. Soften the onion in ¼ cup butter and place some of it in the bottom of a baking dish. Put the sliced potato on top and season. Put the cod steaks on top of the potatoes and cover with the rest of the onions and the bacon.

▲ Place in the oven. After 15 minutes, pour the cream into the dish, dot with 2 tbsp butter and return to the oven for another 40 minutes.

▲ Cover with parsley and serve with Potato Cakes (*see* recipe) and a green salad. This dish is also good cooked without the cream, but it must be covered with foil from the beginning of the cooking.

Fish Steaks with Mussels
COOKING TIME: 30 MINUTES

▲ Dip the fish steaks in seasoned flour and fry them in 2 tbsp of olive oil. Keep warm.

▲ Skin and chop the tomatoes. Chop the onion and the garlic and cook in the remainder of the olive oil and ¼ cup butter. Then add the white wine and simmer for a while.

▲ Add the cleaned mussels and cover with a lid. Cook over a high heat until the mussels have opened. Shake the pan from time to time during the cooking. Take off the flame and remove the mussels and keep with the fish. Put the pan back on the heat and reduce the sauce a little.

▲ Add the rest of the butter cubes and beat until melted, then add the cooked rice and heat through. Shake the pan again while heating.

▲ Put the fish steaks on a serving dish and cover with the mixture. Arrange the mussels in their shells on top and garnish with chopped parsley.

INGREDIENTS
4 large firm, white fish steaks, such as cod or hake

Seasoned flour

⅔ cup virgin olive oil

2 lb ripe tomatoes, or 2 cans chopped tomatoes

1 large Spanish onion

4 large garlic cloves

½ cup unsalted butter, cut into cubes

1 glass dry white wine

2¼ cups mussels, cleaned and debearded

1½ cups cooked rice

Chopped fresh parsley

FOOD FROM THE SEA

No part of Ireland is more than 60 miles from the sea and consequently fish and other sea foods are very much part of the Irish culinary tradition. On many a country inn counter, you will find a saucer of some variety of seaweed, put there for you to chew on, while, on the coast itself – especially in Donegal – modern fishing has meant a new level of prosperity. A walk around the harbor at Killybegs, Ireland's premier fishing port, shows you exactly how life has changed, with huge deep-sea trawlers lining up with small inshore boats to roam the seas from Donegal Bay to Norway.

Smoked Fish Pie

COOKING TIME: 20 MINUTES

INGREDIENTS

2½ *cups béchamel sauce
(see* Basic Recipes)

1 glass dry white wine

2 tbsp cream

¾ lb Finnan haddie, cooked, boned and skinned (other firm-fleshed, smoked fish can be used)

6 oz shrimp tails, cooked

¾ cup cooked button mushrooms

1 tbsp chopped fresh chives and parsley

Salt and pepper

¾ lb flaky or puff pastry dough
(see Basic Recipes) or 2 lb well-flavored mashed potatoes

Milk or egg, to glaze

OVEN TEMPERATURE: 425°F-450°F

▲ Preheat the oven. Pour the béchamel sauce into a bowl. Add the wine and cream, then mix in all the other ingredients, except for the salt and pepper, puff pastry and the glaze.

▲ Season to taste and place in a buttered, deep baking dish. Cover with puff pastry dough. Glaze with milk or a beaten egg, and place in a very hot oven for 15-20 minutes. Serve straight from the dish.

▲ As an alternative to the puff pastry topping, cover the fish mixture with a layer of creamy, seasoned mashed potato, and dot with nuggets of butter.

Sea Bass Cooked with Seaweed in a Paper Case

COOKING TIME: 30 MINUTES

INGREDIENTS

3 lb sea bass

Salt and pepper

1 tbsp each chopped root fennel, shallot and fresh herbs

1 lb fresh seaweed (see Seaweed)

1 glass dry white wine

FOR THE SAUCE:

2 tomatoes (plum type, if available)

1 sweet red pepper

1 bulb of fennel

2 tbsp chopped fresh herbs – parsley, chives, chervil, fennel and tarragon

Lemon juice

Olive oil

Salt and pepper to taste

OVEN TEMPERATURE: 400°F

▲ Preheat the oven. Gut, clean and season the sea bass.
▲ Place the chopped fennel, shallot and herbs in the middle of the fish. Wrap the fish in fresh seaweed and put in a package of wax paper. Before you close the paper package, sprinkle the sea bass with the white wine.
▲ Place on a cookie sheet in the oven for about 30 minutes.
▲ While the fish is cooking, skin and chop the tomatoes. Roast the pepper under the broiler, peel and chop it finely. Chop the fennel into small pieces and combine with the tomatoes, pepper and herbs in a bowl. Mix well and add some lemon juice, olive oil, salt and pepper.
▲ Serve the sea bass hot on a bed of seaweed with the sauce in a separate bowl.

TOP *Fishermen inspect their nets preparatory to a day's trawling;* RIGHT, *gathering seaweed – a common sight in 19th-century times and still a traditional delicacy.*

Skate with Brown-Butter Sauce

COOKING TIME: 20 MINUTES

INGREDIENTS

2 lb skate wings or any flat fish fillets
¼ cup white wine vinegar
4-6 tbsp unsalted butter
1 tbsp chopped capers
Black pepper and salt to taste
Parsley and lemon wedges

▲ Poach the skate wings in water which has a few drops of vinegar in it for 10-15 minutes.
▲ Drain the fish and remove the skin – it comes off very easily at this stage. Keep warm in a low oven.
▲ Melt the butter in the pan over a medium heat until it turns brown – toss in the capers, then add the remaining vinegar. Cook very fast for 30 seconds, then pour over the fish.
▲ Garnish with parsley and lemon wedges, and serve with small new potatoes to soak up the delicious butter.

Flounder with Mustard Sauce

COOKING TIME: 20 MINUTES

INGREDIENTS

4 flounder fillets
2 shallots, chopped
2 tbsp Dijon mustard
⅔ cup light cream
Watercress

OVEN TEMPERATURE: 350°F

▲ Preheat the oven. Butter a baking dish. Place the fish fillets in the dish.
▲ Mix the shallots, mustard and cream together. Pour over the fish and bake in a medium oven for 15-20 minutes.
▲ Serve with bunches of watercress.

ABOVE *Bantry Bay, in Cork, is another favorite fishing ground. Here, try your luck and spend an evening mackerel fishing from a quiet seaside harbor – marvelous sport and a wonderfully fresh, tasty catch.*

Flounder with Mustard Sauce

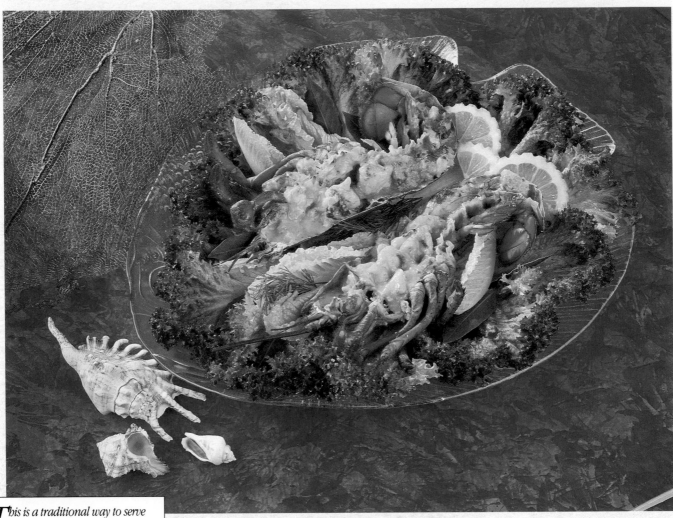

This is a traditional way to serve fresh lobster. It is essential to make it with raw lobster. Get your fish merchant to kill the lobster, cut it lengthwise, and remove all the meat, including the claw meat. This is difficult to do on your own at home. Make sure you keep the coral. This recipe serves two.

Dublin Lawyer

COOKING TIME: 10 MINUTES

INGREDIENTS

6 tbsp butter

1 fresh lobster, about 2½ lb, cut into chunks, together with the coral

4 tbsp Irish whiskey

⅔ cup light cream

Salt and pepper

Lettuce or boiled rice

▲ Heat the butter in a heavy pan until it froths, but do not brown it.

▲ Add the lobster meat and coral and cook lightly for a few minutes.

▲ Warm the whiskey, set it alight and flame the lobster.

▲ When the flames die down, add the cream. Heat for a few moments – on no account allow it to boil.

▲ Place the meat and sauce back into the lobster shells. Season. Serve on a bed of chilled lettuce or on a bed of boiled rice.

> *Brown bread and lots of napkins are needed to enjoy these to the full – eat them with your fingers.*

Dublin Bay Prawns in Garlic Butter

COOKING TIME: 10 MINUTES

INGREDIENTS

1½ lb live jumbo shrimp with shells

½ cup garlic butter (made with unsalted butter), melted

Lemon wedges

Parsley sprigs

▲ Boil some water and salt in a large pan. Plunge the shrimp in the water Bring back to a boil and cook for 1 minute.

▲ Drain the shrimp and toss in hot garlic butter for 2-3 minutes. Serve garnished with lemon wedges and parsley.

Preparing Crab

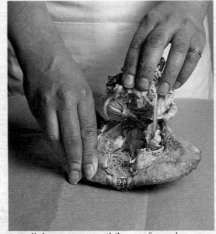

1 Turn the crab onto its back. Twist off the claws and then the legs – do not pull them.

2 Pull the apron or tail flap up from the pointed end to remove the intestinal vein and the body from the shell.

3 Remove the "dead men's fingers" – these are the soft and spongy gills you will find at the sides of the body. Remove the stomach sac – this lies behind the head.

4 Prise out any cartilaginous membrane from the shell and discard it.

5 Remove the brown meat from the shell and keep to one side.

6 Using your thumbs, break the shell to enlarge and neaten the opening, if wished. Wash the shell thoroughly.

7 Remove the white meat from the body, claws and legs. Use a hammer or crackers to open the claws and legs. A skewer is also useful for extracting flesh from awkward corners.

Creamed Crab

Deviled Crab (for 4)

COOKING TIME: 15-20 MINUTES

INGREDIENTS

4 cooked crabs

½ cup butter, melted

2 cups fresh bread crumbs

1 heaped tbsp Dijon mustard

Lemon juice

Pinch of cayenne pepper

OVEN TEMPERATURE: 350°F

▲ Preheat the oven. Remove all the meat from the freshly cooked crabs (*see* Preparing Crab for method).

▲ Place the meat in a mixing bowl with the melted butter and fresh bread crumbs. Add the mustard, lemon juice and cayenne. Mix very well.

▲ Stuff the mixture back into the crab shells and heat in a very hot oven for 15 minutes, then finish under the broiler for a few minutes more. Serve very hot with lemon wedges.

Creamed Crab

PREPARATION TIME: 20 MINUTES

INGREDIENTS

½ lb freshly cooked crab meat

2 tomatoes, peeled and chopped

2 hard-cooked eggs, chopped

1¼ cups Green Mayonnaise
(see Basic Recipes)

Juice of 1 lemon

Chopped fresh chives and parsley

Salt and pepper

▲ Put all the ingredients in a bowl and mix well. Serve with chilled pieces of Romaine lettuce, or in puff pastry patty shells.

INGREDIENTS

2 lb Finnan haddie or smoked cod
1 bay leaf
4 cups long grain or basmati rice
1 cup unsalted butter
8 hard-cooked eggs
1 tbsp good curry powder
1¼ cups béchamel sauce
(see Basic Recipes)
Chopped fresh cilantro
Lemon slices

Kedgeree

COOKING TIME: 30 MINUTES

▲ Cover the fish with cold water and add the bay leaf. Bring to a boil and turn off the heat. Remove the fish and keep the water.

▲ Cook the rice in ½ cup butter and the fish water, adding extra cold water, if necessary. There should be double the volume of water to rice. Cook the rice until most of the water has been absorbed and holes appear on the surface. Turn off the heat and cover – leave in a warm place or low oven until you deal with the fish.

▲ Remove all bones and skin from the fish. Shell and roughly chop the eggs. Melt the rest of the butter and add the curry powder. Cook for a couple of minutes, then add the fish.

▲ Make the béchamel sauce (*see* Basic Recipes) and add to the fish and butter. Cook for 2 minutes. Then gently fold into the rice, which should now be perfectly cooked, making sure all the grains are equally coated. Mix in the chopped hard-cooked eggs.

▲ Serve in a large, warm bowl, garnished with fresh cilantro and lemon slices.

Kedgeree is an Anglo-Indian dish which is good for breakfast, lunch or supper. In Ireland, I remember it mainly as a breakfast dish – served on Sundays in country houses. It has happily outlasted the colonial connections.

Soused Herrings with Sour Cream

PREPARATION AND COOKING TIME:
20 MINUTES + COOLING

6 fresh herring fillets

1 large Spanish onion, thinly sliced

6 bay leaves

18 whole black peppercorns

1¼ cups red-wine vinegar and water mixed

1¼ cups sour cream

Chopped fresh drill

OVEN TEMPERATURE: 325°F

▲ Preheat the oven. Wash the herring fillets and pat them dry with paper towels.

▲ Place some of the thinly sliced onion, a bay leaf and 3 whole peppercorns on each fish. Roll up the herrings with the tail-end away from you. Place in a baking dish and cover with the vinegar and water mixture.

▲ Place in a medium oven until the herrings are cooked – about 20 minutes. Let the fish cool in the liquid for several hours or overnight.

▲ Serve cold with a spoonful of sour cream, garnished with chopped dill.

Meat Dishes

LEFT
The luscious pastures of County
Cork – ideal country for raising
dairy and beef cattle, as well
as sheep.

4 lb beef standing rib roast
Sea salt and freshly ground black pepper
½ cup unsalted butter

Roast Rib of Beef with
Béarnaise Sauce

COOKING TIME: 40 MINUTES

1 cup unsalted butter,
cut into cubes
4 shallots or scallions, finely chopped
3 tbsp white-wine vinegar
2 tbsp chopped fresh tarragon
½ tsp chopped fresh chervil
Pinch of ground black pepper and salt
4 egg yolks
2 tbsp cold water

OVEN TEMPERATURE: 425°F

▲ Season the rib of beef with salt and pepper and place in a heavy roasting pan. Melt the butter and cook in a hot oven, browning the meat on both sides. For rare meat, cook for 10 minutes per pound on each side. Remove the meat to a serving platter and keep warm.

▲ To make the sauce, in a small heavy saucepan melt 1 tbsp of butter. Add the shallots. Cook slowly for about 10 minutes, then add the vinegar, half the tarragon and chervil, and salt and pepper to taste. Reduce the sauce to about 2 tsp.

▲ Cool the mixture and add the egg yolks and the cold water. Mix with a whisk over a low heat or in a double boiler or bowl over saucepan of boiling water. Make sure you amalgamate the eggs with the shallot mixture, but do not cook them or the sauce will be ruined.

▲ When the egg yolks look thick and creamy, gradually whisk in the remaining butter, making sure the sauce does not separate. If it gets too thick, add a little water.

▲ When the sauce is finished, add more chopped tarragon and chervil. Keep warm in the double boiler or bowl above saucepan of boiling water. (If the worst happens and the sauce separates, start again with a little water in a saucepan. Heat it continuously, adding small quantities of the sauce until it emulsifies again.)

▲ Carve the ribs and serve the sauce separately.

ABOVE *Irish whiskey, with a kick all of its own, is a superb aperitif for pre-meal drinking.*

Gaelic Steak

▲ Rub each side of the steak with the garlic butter. Place on a hot griddle or in a large skillet over a high heat. For rare steak, cook on each side for 3 minutes; allow 4 minutes each side for a medium steak and 5 minutes if you prefer your steak well-done.

▲ Then pour a shot of warmed whiskey over the steak and set alight. When the flames die down, put the steak on a hot plate.

▲ Add a little cream to the pan juices and cook over a fierce heat for a few minutes. Pour the sauce over the steak, season and serve with sprigs of watercress.

INGREDIENTS

½ lb sirloin steak per person
Garlic butter
Shot of Irish whiskey
Cream
Salt and pepper
Watercress

I *don't know if this dish was named after the Duke of Wellington or happened to be something he liked. It is rather an ersatz Irish dish as the Duke of Wellington was merely born in Ireland. However, it makes a very good hot or cold party dish.*

Beef Wellington

INGREDIENTS

1 lb flaky or puff pastry dough (see Basic Recipes)

2-lb beef tender loin, in 1 piece

Salt and pepper

¾ cup butter

2½ cups mushrooms

1 medium onion

2 garlic cloves

Mixed fresh herbs

1 egg, beaten, to glaze

OVEN TEMPERATURE: 425°F

PREPARATION AND COOKING TIME:
30 MINUTES

▲ Preheat the oven. Make the pastry dough (*see* Basic Recipes) and chill in the refrigerator.

▲ Trim the beef and season with salt and pepper. Rub with butter and roast in a hot oven for about 10 minutes.

▲ Finely chop the mushrooms, onion, garlic and herbs and cook in the rest of the butter. Drain well and put in a layer on the top of the beef.

▲ Roll out the dough large enough to fit around the beef and meet at the top. Brush beaten egg on the edges of the dough and squeeze together with your fingers. If you are worried about the dough opening during cooking, put the seam under the beef and decorate the top with dough leaves made from the trimmings. Brush all over with beaten egg and roast for about 20 minutes or until the pastry is golden. Serve hot or cold.

ABOVE *My goodness, my Guinness! This is Ireland's world-famous stout, hugely popular at home, (where it still comes in traditional wooden casks), and abroad.*

Beef in Guinness

COOKING TIME: ABOUT 2 HOURS

INGREDIENTS

2-3 lb beef for braising
Seasoned flour
Oil or dripping
2 onions, sliced
4 garlic cloves, whole
3 carrots, sliced
1 large bunch of fresh herbs
Salt and pepper
Beef broth (see Basic Recipes)
2 bottles of Guinness
1 oyster per person (optional)

▲ Cut the beef into large chunks and dip in seasoned flour. Fry in hot oil or dripping. Fry and brown the onions and garlic.

▲ Place the meat, onions and other vegetables in a casserole dish. Add the herbs and seasoning, and cover with beef broth. Bring to a boil, then cover and cook over a low heat for 1½ hours. Add the Guinness, bring to a boil and simmer for another 30 minutes.

▲ Lift the meat out of the sauce with a slotted spoon and serve; reduce the sauce to half the quantity over a high heat. Pour it over the beef again, season to taste, and add the oysters, if liked.

▲ Serve with wedges of white crusty bread with mustard and a pint of Guinness.

ABOVE *Ireland's dairy and beef cattle need careful nurturing to maintain their quality. The hay here will be used as winter fodder.*

---

*S*piced beef is traditional Christmas fare in Ireland.
As a child I remember it appearing in the butchers'shops a few weeks before Christmas, looking like chocolate logs decorated with holly and red ribbons. It is, however, very simple to prepare.

INGREDIENTS

20 cloves
2 pieces of mace
2 tsp ground allspice or cinnamon
6 shallots
2 tsp saltpetre (preserving agent)
2 tbsp brown sugar
1 lb coarse sea salt
1 tsp black pepper
7-8 lb joint of beef
2-3 bay leaves
Grated nutmeg
2 bottles Guinness or brown beer

Irish Spiced Beef

PREPARATION AND COOKING TIME:
AT LEAST 8 DAYS + 5-6 HOURS

▲ Put all the spices in a coffee grinder and grind to a powder.
▲ Put the shallots, spices, saltpetre, sugar, salt and peppered meat in a shallow earthenware or strong glass dish. Rub the salt and spices into the meat, grate nutmeg over it, and leave for a week in a cool place.
▲ Turn the meat once a day and rub the spices into the meat again.
▲ After at least a week, wrap the meat in cheesecloth and simmer in hot water for 5-6 hours with the bay leaves and nutmeg. About 30 minutes before the end of the cooking, add 2 bottles of Guinness or brown beer.
▲ When cooked, remove from the liquid and cool, pressed between 2 plates for several hours or overnight. Serve thinly sliced. It is always served cold on Christmas Eve or St Stephen's Day (26 December).

> *Like smoked ham, salt beef needs to be soaked in cold water the night before cooking.*

Salt Beef with Cabbage and Parsley Sauce

PREPARATION AND COOKING TIME:
OVERNIGHT + 2 HOURS

INGREDIENTS

6 lb corned brisket of beef
1 Savoy or curly cabbage, shredded
1 onion, coarsely chopped
2 bay leaves
Parsley sauce (see *Béchamel Sauce*)

▲ Discard the soaking water, then put the beef into a large pan and cover with fresh cold water. Bring to a boil and throw the water away, then cover with more fresh cold water.

▲ Poach with the onion and bay leaves for about 2 hours. Ten minutes before the end of the cooking, add the shredded Savoy or curly cabbage.

▲ Remove the beef, cut into slices and arrange on a hot platter. Surround with the drained cabbage and cover with parsley sauce.

▲ On a separate tray, serve pickled cucumbers and mustard.

MAGIC CRYSTAL
FROM WATERFORD

At the Waterford Crystal factory, the dream of reviving Ireland's 19th-century glass-making tradition has been fully realized, as the showroom examples here demonstrate. The sign (RIGHT) indicates the number of foreign visitors the factory attracts.

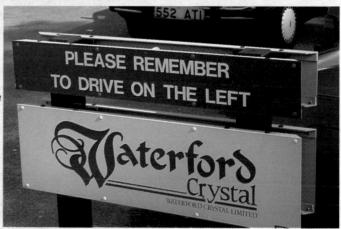

Beef Stew with Herb Dumplings

COOKING TIME: 2 HOURS 30 MINUTES

INGREDIENTS

2 lb chuck beef, cut into large chunks
Seasoned flour
Beef dripping, fat or oil
2 onions, chopped
2 carrots, chopped
2 garlic cloves, chopped
1 turnip, peeled and chopped
2 celery stalks, chopped
2 tomatoes, peeled, seeded and chopped
3 floury potatoes, peeled and chopped
1 large bunch of fresh herbs
Salt, pepper, whole allspice berries
2½ cups beef broth (see Basic Recipes)

▲ Dip the meat into seasoned flour, then seal in hot beef dripping or oil. Then fry the onions and the rest of the vegetables.

▲ Place the meat on a bed of vegetables in a large saucepan or casserole. Stuff the bunch of herbs in the middle, season and cover with well-flavored beef broth. Cover and cook over a low heat for 2 hours.

▲ While the stew is cooking make the dumplings, first by mixing all the dry ingredients together, then by adding the beaten egg to bind.

▲ Divide the mixture into small pieces, about the size of a walnut. Roll between floured palms into even shapes.

▲ Cook in boiling broth or salted water for 15-20 minutes, then add to the stew 15-20 minutes before it is fully cooked.

▲ Serve on a hot plate, garnished with parsley.

TO MAKE THE DUMPLINGS:

COOKING TIME: 20 MINUTES

6 tbsp self rising flour
1 cup fresh bread crumbs
¼ cup grated suet, preferably vegetarian
1 tbsp or to taste chopped mixed fresh herbs
Salt and pepper
Finely chopped shallots (optional)
1 egg, beaten
Broth or water

Rack of Lamb in a Mustard Crust with Mint Sauce or Jelly

PREPARATION AND COOKING TIME: 25 MINUTES

2 well-trimmed racks of lamb – allow 3 chops per portion

½ cup butter

4 cups fresh bread crumbs

2 tbsp Dijon mustard

1 tsp rosemary

1 onion, finely chopped

Mint sauce, or 1 tbsp mint or red currant jelly per person

OVEN TEMPERATURE: 425°F

▲ Preheat the oven. Make sure any surplus fat is trimmed from the meat.

▲ Make the crust by melting the butter and mixing all the other ingredients, except the mint sauce, into it. Allow the mixture to chill in the refrigerator for about 15 minutes. Cut the racks of lamb into portions. Coat the back of the chops with a layer of crust about ½ in thick.

▲ Place the racks in a roasting pan in a hot oven for about 10 minutes.

▲ Serve with mint sauce, mint jelly or red currant jelly.

This recipe is a classic Irish stew. Paul Bocuse describes it as one of the world's great classic dishes. It is a white stew and should not even have carrots in it, although carrots or braised red cabbage are the traditional accompaniments.

Irish Stew
COOKING TIME: 3 HOURS

▲ Preheat the oven, if using. In a large heavy pan or flameproof casserole place one-third of the sliced onions and the sliced potatoes. On this layer place half of the meat, season, and add half of the remaining onions and the sliced potatoes. Season and add the garlic, herbs and the rest of the meat. Finish with a layer of the sliced onions and potatoes, and season with more salt and pepper. Just cover the meat and vegetables with water, bring to a boil and cover with wax paper and a lid. Cook slowly on top of the stove or in a low oven for 1 hour.

▲ Peel the new potatoes and the pearl onions.

▲ Take the stew from the oven or off the heat after 1 hour – the onions and the potatoes should be almost falling apart. Mash them a little bit and add the new potatoes and whole onions to the stew.

▲ The meat may be removed now and put back in again before the end of cooking to prevent it falling off the bone; this is for aesthetic purposes only, as it does not affect the flavor. At this point if the stew is too thick add some water. Cover again and cook for another hour. Garnish with parsley and serve with carrots or braised red cabbage.

INGREDIENTS

2 lb onions, sliced

2 lb floury potatoes, peeled and sliced

3 lb neck of lamb

Salt and pepper

3 garlic cloves

Fresh parsley, thyme, celery tops and bay leaf tied together

12 small new potatoes

12 pearl onions

Chopped fresh parsley

OVEN TEMPERATURE, IF USED: 300°F

RIGHT *Irish lamb perfectly complements the other ingredients in classic stews and casseroles.*

One of the reasons why this excellent dish is rarely seen today is probably due to the scarcity of mutton. Mutton is now considered the poor relation of lamb. I don't see the reason for this, as I consider it has a much better flavor, and is as good hot or cold. A side product of poaching the mutton in the following recipe is a wonderful mutton broth (see *Mutton Broth with Barley*).

Mutton in Caper Sauce

COOKING TIME: 2 HOURS 20 MINUTES

▲ Make sure there is no surplus fat on the meat. Put into a deep, heavy saucepan and cover with cold water. Bring slowly to a boil, then simmer for about 15 minutes. Skim off any scum that appears on the surface.

▲ Add the scrubbed and peeled vegetables, herbs and seasoning. Cover and simmer gently for about 2 hours.

▲ Make the sauce by melting the butter and adding the flour to make a roux. Cook for 1 minute. Add the strained broth from the meat pan, gradually stirring to avoid lumps. Boil for 3 minutes, then add the capers. Season with salt and pepper. (Be careful with the salt as the capers may be salty enough – I once nearly poisoned people by adding extra salt when the capers had been preserved in brine.)

▲ Finally, add some cream and heat, but do not boil again.

▲ Serve the mutton cut into thick slices on a platter. Cover with the caper sauce and serve with the cooked vegetables.

INGREDIENTS

1 boned and rolled leg of lamb or mutton, about 4 lb in weight

2 lb whole tiny carrots, scrubbed

2 lb pearl onions

1 lb small turnips

2 garlic cloves

Bunch of fresh thyme, rosemary and bay leaf

Salt and pepper

FOR THE SAUCE:

2 tbsp butter

2 tbsp all purpose flour

2½ cups mutton broth (see recipe)

Small jar capers

Light cream

Salt and pepper

Coddle was traditionally served when "the Men" came in from the pub on a Saturday night.

Dublin Coddle

COOKING TIME: ABOUT 1 HOUR

INGREDIENTS

2 lb thick pure pork link sausages
Seasoned flour
A little bacon fat or sunflower oil
2 large onions, sliced
2 garlic cloves
1 lb bacon slices, or knuckle of ham
4 large potatoes, thickly sliced
2 carrots, thickly sliced
Bunch of fresh herbs
Black pepper
Hard cider
Chopped parsley

▲ Dip the sausages into seasoned flour and seal in hot bacon fat or oil. Soften the onions and whole garlic cloves in the oil.

▲ Place the sausages, bacon and onions in a large saucepan with thickly sliced potatoes and carrots. Bury a large bunch of fresh herbs in the middle and cover with cider.

▲ Cook over a moderate heat for at least an hour, but do not boil.

▲ Garnish with parsley. Serves 6 in deep dishes, together with soda bread. Wash down with mugs of Guinness.

The night before using the ham, soak it in cold water to remove the surplus salt. Saw off the knuckle and use for broth.
The prunes must also be soaked the night before.

Braised Ham with Prunes

PREPARATION AND COOKING TIME:
OVERNIGHT + 2 HOURS

INGREDIENTS

6 lb smoked (Limerick) ham, lightly cured
1 lb large whole prunes
1 apple, stuck with cloves
Juniper berries
2½ cups hard cider

OVEN TEMPERATURE: 350°F

▲ Preheat the oven. Remove the ham from the cold water and place in a large pan with fresh cold water. Bring slowly to a boil, then throw the water away.

▲ Place in a casserole or deep baking dish, surrounded by the drained prunes, apple and juniper berries. Pour the cider over the ham and loosely cover with foil. Cook in a medium oven, basting every 15 minutes. Allow 20 minutes to the 1 lb (about 2 hours).

▲ Remove the skin when the ham is cooked. Serve the ham on a plate with a few prunes and some parsley or onion sauce (*see* Béchamel Sauce and Soft Cooked Eggs in Ramekins with Onion Sauce).

Pork steak is a cut of meat once unique to Ireland, but it may now be found under the name pork tenderloin. It is lean and moist and is at its best stuffed and roast.
I like to use about 2 lb of pork tenderloin left whole.

Roast Stuffed Pork

COOKING TIME: 1 HOUR 15 MINUTES

INGREDIENTS

2 lb pork tenderloin

Salt

2 tbsp butter

2 tbsp hard cider or water

FOR THE STUFFING:

4½ cups mashed potato

¼ cup butter

1 onion, finely chopped

2 large cooking apples

Handful chopped fresh sage and thyme

Salt and pepper

OVEN TEMPERATURE: 350°F

▲ Make the stuffing first. Mash the potatoes. Add the butter, chopped onion, chopped apple, herbs, salt and pepper. Mix well and check the seasoning.

▲ Place the meat in a ring shape in a casserole or roasting pan. Put the stuffing in the middle. Rub the meat with salt and butter and put a little cider or water in the pan. Cover loosely with foil and place in a medium oven for about 1 hour.

▲ This dish is marvelous hot or cold and may be served with roasted apples. Serve cut into little medallions with the stuffing and a roasted apple. The pan juices may be reduced and poured over the medallions. It makes a good alternative to turkey or roast beef for Christmas dinner and goes very well with root vegetables.

ABOVE *The smart check frontage of this Kilkenny victualers complements the fresh meat to be found in its cool interior.*

Pork Ciste

COOKING TIME: 2 HOURS

INGREDIENTS

6 lean pork chops
2 pork kidneys
1 large onion
2 carrots
¼ cup butter
⅓ cup raisins and golden raisins
1 tbsp chopped fresh parsley
1 tbsp chopped fresh sage and thyme
Salt and pepper
Approx 2½ cups broth or cider

SUET CRUST

1½ cups self-rising flour
Pinch of salt
½ cup grated suet or vegetarian suet
⅔ cup milk
Pinch of cardamom seeds, crushed
1 tbsp grated cooking apple
1 tsp apple pie spice

▲ Trim any fat off the pork chops. Peel and cut any tubes off the kidneys and slice them. Peel and slice the vegetables.

▲ Fry the meat in the butter over a high heat, without burning the butter. Remove to a casserole dish, then fry the vegetables.

▲ Arrange the chops around the edge of the casserole dish, arranging the kidneys and the vegetables in the middle with the dried fruit, herbs and seasoning. Add enough broth or cider to cover the vegetables. Cover with a lid, bring to a boil and simmer for 30 minutes.

▲ Make the suet pastry dough. Mix all the dry ingredients in a bowl and add the milk. Knead into a fairly stiff dough, then roll it out to fit into the casserole dish and press it down over the meat and vegetables. Cover with wax paper and a lid. Simmer for 1½ hours.

▲ To serve, loosen around the pastry lid and cut into 6 portions. Place 1 chop and some kidney and vegetable mixture on each plate with the crust, or *ciste,* on top. *Ciste* (pronounced kishte) merely means "cake" in Irish.

Poultry and Game

Poached Turkey with
Celery Sauce   76

Michaelmas Goose with Red Cabbage,
Apple and Chestnuts   77

Chicken and Mushroom Pie   78

Wild Duck with Spiced Oranges   79

Game Pie   80

Pigeon and Bacon Pie with
Stuffed Apples   81

Braised Pheasant with Apple and
Cream Sauce   82

Hare Pudding   83

LEFT
*Ducks, with other poultry, are all
part and parcel of the typical Irish
farm scene.*

Turkey tends to be very dry, a problem this recipe overcomes. It makes a very welcome change from the ubiquitous roast stuffed turkey.

Poached Turkey with Celery Sauce

COOKING TIME: 4 HOURS + 15 MINUTES

INGREDIENTS

Giblet broth
10-12 lb turkey
1 lb bacon slices, cubed
4 carrots, sliced
4 small onions, stuck with cloves
1 celery stalk, chopped
Bunch of fresh herbs
Assorted vegetables
Watercress or fresh Italian parsley
to garnish

FOR THE SAUCE:

2 tbsp butter
2 tbsp all purpose flour
2½ cups turkey broth (see Basic Recipes)
1 large head celery, boiled and chopped
1 tbsp chopped fresh parsley
Light cream

OVEN TEMPERATURE: 350°F

▲ Make a broth from the giblets, or use some white broth (*see* Basic Recipes). Wipe the turkey inside and out. In a very large pan, heat the bacon and vegetables.

▲ Place the turkey on top of the vegetables, cover with the broth and drop in the herbs. Cook the bird very slowly for 4 hours. Turn it a couple of times during the cooking. When it is ready, keep in a warm oven.

▲ For the sauce, make a roux with the butter and flour. Slowly add the strained turkey stock and stir while bringing this to a boil. Boil for about 3 minutes, then add the celery and parsley. Finish with a little cream, but do not boil.

▲ Take the turkey from the oven and remove the skin. Cut the turkey into pieces and serve on a platter with other cooked vegetables, including Brussels sprouts, pearl onions, carrots or other preferred vegetables.

▲ Pour the celery sauce over the turkey and garnish.

Michaelmas Goose with Red Cabbage, Apple and Chestnuts

COOKING TIME: ABOUT 2 ½ HOURS

INGREDIENTS	FOR RED CABBAGE:
1 young goose, about 8-10 lb	1 Spanish onion
Salt	1 red cabbage
1 tbsp goose or duck fat	¼ cup unsalted butter
Seasoned flour	½ lb cooked chestnuts
FOR STUFFING:	2 cooking apples
2 lb potatoes	Salt, pepper, 5 juniper berries
2 onions, chopped	Hard cider or water
Goose liver, chopped	FOR APPLE SAUCE:
2 tbsp butter	3 cooking apples
1 bunch of scallions	1 tbsp brown sugar
1 tsp each chopped thyme and sage	1 tbsp butter
Salt and pepper	Grated orange zest

OVEN TEMPERATURE: 350°F

▲ First make the stuffing. Scrub the potatoes and boil in salted water in their skins. Peel and mash them while they are still hot.

▲ Soften the onions and liver in the butter. Add to the mashed potatoes, then sprinkle over the scallions, herbs and seasoning. Add a lot of freshly ground black pepper.

▲ Clean out the goose and wipe with paper towel. Put the stuffing in the belly of the bird and sew up the vent with thick sewing thread. (If you are cooking a goose at Christmas, it is a different beast and very fat – cook the stuffing separately in a baking dish.) Rub the salt and fat over the goose and place in a roasting pan with 2 tbsp water.

▲ Roast in a medium oven for 2 hours. Baste from time to time. In the last half hour, dredge with flour and allow to become crisp. (If you are cooking a goose at Christmas, you do not need to baste it – as it has a lot of fat. Cook it on a wire rack above a roasting pan to catch the fat dripping from the bird.)

▲ To make the traditional red cabbage, slice the onion and shred the cabbage. Heat in the butter in a large pot until soft. Add the cooked and peeled chestnuts together with the apples. Put the pot in the oven with the goose. Add the seasoning and a little water or cider and serve with the goose and apple sauce.

▲ Apple sauce is always served with goose in Ireland. Peel and core the apples. Heat 2 tbsp water and sugar together in a saucepan, then add the apples. Boil until they disintegrate. Mash, add the butter and grated orange zest, mix well and return to a boiling point.

LEFT *Since medieval times, geese have been a traditional Irish favourite, though today they are a rich man's, rather than a poor man's, luxury.*

INGREDIENTS

1 good-sized boiling chicken

1 Spanish onion

Fresh parsley, thyme and bay leaf tied together

Carrots, celery and leeks

Dry white wine (optional)

1 lb button mushrooms, or wild mushrooms, if available

Knob of butter, softened and worked with 1 tbsp all purpose flour

1 tbsp chopped fresh herbs, including tarragon

1 lb flaky pastry dough (see Basic Recipes)

1 egg, beaten, to glaze

OVEN TEMPERATURE: 425°F

Chicken and Mushroom Pie

COOKING TIME: 1 HOUR 30 MINUTES

▲ Place the chicken in a pot with the onion, bouquet garni and vegetables. Cover with water and some dry white wine, if you have any.

▲ When the chicken is cooked, remove it from the pot and reserve the broth. Take off all the skin and remove the bones and any tough sinews. Cut the chicken into bite-sized pieces.

▲ Sauté the mushrooms in a little butter. Remove from the butter and place in a deep, baking dish together with the prepared chicken.

▲ Into the pan juices from the mushrooms, gradually add 2½ cups or more of the reserved chicken broth. Cook for a few minutes over a high heat. Thicken with a knob of butter worked together with 1 tbsp of flour. Add the fresh herbs and seasoning and pour over the chicken and mushrooms.

▲ Roll out the flaky pastry dough. Cover the contents to the edges of the baking dish, and brush an egg glaze on the pie. Cook in a hot oven until golden brown.

In common with other game birds, wild duck must be hung for about three days, until the skin has a greenish tinge to it.

As well as oranges, tiny Clementines are delicious treated this way. Keep the spiced fruit for about two months before using.

Wild Duck with Spiced Oranges

COOKING TIME: 40-45 MINUTES

INGREDIENTS

2 wild duck
¼ cup butter
1¼ cups port, warmed
Juice of 1 orange
Salt and freshly ground pepper
Bunch of watercress
OVEN TEMPERATURE: 400°F
FOR THE SPICED ORANGES:

10 large thin-skinned oranges
2½ cups white-wine vinegar
6½ cups sugar
2 cinnamon sticks
¼ tsp ground cloves
6 blades of mace

▲ Preheat the oven. Rub the birds with butter and roast in a hot oven for 30 minutes, or 20 minutes to cook "pink." Add the warmed port and put back in the oven for 10 minutes. Remove the birds from the pan to a serving platter and keep warm. Add the orange juice to the pan and cook over a fierce heat until the liquid is reduced.

▲ Pour the juices over the birds and decorate with sprigs of watercress. Serve with spiced oranges.

▲ To make the oranges, slice them about ¼ in thick. Lay them in a pan or skillet and just cover with water.

▲ Simmer until the orange peel is tender, then take off the heat. In a saucepan, put the vinegar, sugar and spices and boil together for about 10 minutes.

▲ Drain the oranges and keep the liquid. Lay half the oranges in the syrup, making sure it covers the slices. Simmer for 30-40 minutes, until the fruit turns clear. Lift out into a dish, and put the remaining oranges into the pan. If the syrup does not cover them, add some of the orange cooking liquid. Cook as before.

▲ Turn everything into a glass bowl and leave overnight. If the syrup is thin, remove the oranges with a slotted spoon and boil the liquid in a saucepan until reduced and thick. If the syrup is thick, just bring the fruit and liquid to a boil again and put into clean jars. Tie covers on when cool. If you do not have enough syrup to cover the oranges, boil up some more in the same proportions as before and fill the jars with it.

Serves 8-10. It is not really worth making a game pie for less than eight people.

INGREDIENTS

2-2½ lb venison for stewing, or a mixture of rabbit and venison

8-12 oz pheasant, partridge or pigeon

1 onion

2 leeks

1 turnip

2 carrots

Fresh parsley, thyme and bay leaf tied together

½ cup butter

10 tbsp chopped shallots

3 cups chopped mushrooms

½ lb bacon slices

½ lb veal, ham or pork

¼ lb chicken livers

Game Pie

COOKING TIME: 2 HOURS

▲ First of all make the broth. Put any bones you have, from whichever bird you use, together with the venison trimmings in a pot. Add the onion, leeks, carrots and turnip with enough water to cover. Submerge the herbs and simmer while you prepare the rest of the pie.

▲ In ¼ cup of the butter, fry the jointed birds until cooked "pink." Remove. In a little more butter fry the shallots and mushrooms.

▲ Preheat the oven. Line a 10-12-in deep baking dish with half the bacon slices. Grind the rest of the bacon with the veal, ham or pork. Add the chicken livers and the reserved livers from the birds used in the pie. Put the ground meat into a bowl and mix with the fried shallots and mushrooms, herbs, orange zest, salt, pepper and spices. Add the bread crumbs, the whole egg and the Madeira. Mix well. If the mixture is too dry, add some broth.

▲ Now begin filling the baking dish. Put a layer of the game joints over the bacon slices. Season and sprinkle with parsley. Add a layer of hard-cooked eggs, and then some of the cooked liver mixture rolled into balls. Continue the layers until full, cover with foil and bake for up to 1 hour.

▲ Take out of the oven and cool. If it has gone a bit dry, add some broth. Put a pie funnel in the middle of the filling, cover with the piecrust pastry dough and let some of the funnel protrude. Glaze with egg and cook in a hot oven until the pastry is golden brown. Serve with a fruit jelly.

2 tbsp chopped fresh thyme

Chopped fresh savory, tarragon and parsley

Grated zest of 1 orange

Salt and freshly ground pepper

Pinch of ground cloves

Pinch of grated nutmeg

2 cups fresh bread crumbs

1 egg, beaten

1 glass Madeira or port

5 hard-cooked eggs, chopped

1-1½ lb piecrust pastry dough (see Basic Recipes)

1 egg, beaten, to glaze

OVEN TEMPERATURE: 375°F

ABOVE RIGHT *Irish ingenuity knows no bounds when it comes to food, as this mobile cafeteria, complete with Egon Ronay recommendation, shows.*

Pigeon and Bacon Pie with Stuffed Apples

COOKING TIME: 80 MINUTES

INGREDIENTS

4 pigeons

¼ cup butter

2½ cups broth
(see Basic Recipes)

1 large onion, chopped

3 cups mushrooms, sliced

½ lb bacon slices, chopped

Pepper

4 hard-cooked eggs, chopped

1 tbsp chopped fresh parsley

Marsala or red wine

Piecrust or flaky pastry dough, to cover
(see Basic Recipes)

1 egg, beaten, to glaze

OVEN TEMPERATURE: 425°F, THEN 325°F

▲ Preheat the oven. Cut the pigeons in half and brown in the butter. Simmer for just over 1 hour in the broth.

▲ Sauté the onion, mushrooms and chopped bacon in some butter. Place in a deep baking dish with the drained pigeons. Season with pepper and add the chopped hard-cooked eggs and parsley and enough broth mixed with Marsala or red wine to cover.

▲ Put a rim of the dough of your choice around the edge of the dish. Brush it with beaten egg and cover with a lid of dough. Pinch the edges and decorate with dough leaves. Brush with beaten egg.

▲ Put into a hot oven for 10 minutes to cook the pastry, then reduce the heat and cook for 1 hour. If the pastry looks like it is overcooking, cover with wax paper.

▲ Serve with stuffed apples or fresh pears, if preferred.

Stuffed Apples

INGREDIENTS

6 medium-sized sharp eating apples

Unsalted butter

Brown sugar, ground cloves and apple
pie spice, combined to taste

▲ Core the apples and stuff with a mixture of unsalted butter, brown sugar and spices. Cook with the pigeon pie when the pastry lid goes on.

Braised Pheasant with Apple and Cream Sauce

COOKING TIME: 45-50 MINUTES

INGREDIENTS

1 brace of pheasants
¼ cup butter
Chopped fresh thyme, sage and rosemary
2 cooking apples
2 eating apples
1¼ cups hard cider
1¼ cups light cream or crème fraîche
Salt and pepper
Parsley and chives, to garnish

▲ Brown the pheasants in some of the butter. Remove the pheasants. Cut them in half and rub with the chopped herbs.

▲ Peel and slice the apples, then fry in the rest of the butter. Put the pheasants and the apples in a casserole, and pour over the cider. Cover the casserole and cook for about 40 minutes on the top of the oven.

▲ Remove the pheasants from the liquid and reduce the sauce. Then add the cream and heat just to boiling point, but do not boil unless you are using crème fraîche.

▲ Pour over the pheasants and garnish with parsley and chives.

ABOVE *The Irish love of hunting and other field sports is world renowned and hare coursing is one of the many such activities that take place in suitable countryside.*

Hare Pudding

COOKING TIME: OVER 4 HOURS

INGREDIENTS

6 bacon slices
1 young hare, cut into pieces
Seasoned flour
1 onion, chopped
2 garlic cloves, crushed
Mixed chopped fresh herbs
Salt and freshly ground black pepper
1¼ cups beef or game broth
(see *Basic Recipes*)
1 glass port
Red currant jelly

TO MAKE THE SUET PASTRY:

1½ cups self rising flour
Pinch of salt
¼ lb suet or vegetarian suet, shredded
Cold water

▲ Make the pastry first. Sift the flour and salt together. Add the suet and rub in with the fingers for a couple of minutes. Add cold water until you get a light dough. Knead lightly on a floured surface. Make into a small ball. Roll out and use at once – it does not need to "rest" in the refrigerator.

▲ Roll the pastry out to ¾-in thickness and line a deep, heatproof bowl with it. Line the bottom and sides of the bowl with the bacon. Dip the pieces of hare in seasoned flour and seal in hot fat. Soften the onion and place in the bowl with the pieces of hare. Add the garlic, herbs and seasoning, then cover with the broth and port. Roll out the rest of the suet pastry dough and cover the pudding. Trim the edges and press down well at the join. Cover with wax paper and tie around with string.

▲ Steam or boil for 4 hours. Serve in the bowl with a white napkin tied around it. Pass the red currant jelly in a jug.

Vegetables and Salads

LEFT
*Rich fields, full of produce –
a typically Irish scene. Down to
the smallest cottage, all Irish
country dwellers have their kitchen
garden, while on farms, vegetable
crops are frequently raised on a
commercial scale.*

Seaweed and sea vegetables have been a staple in the Irish diet since prehistoric times. There are written details of dishes using seaweed as far back as the monastic period of the 5th and 6th centuries.

Carrageen, dulse and sloke are the most common seaweeds used in Ireland today.

Carrageen: *Carrageen is also known as "sea moss" or "Irish moss." It is found on the rocks around the coast of Ireland. It is either purple or green, and it grows in short branches. Carrageen is used to thicken soups and mousses, and is a great alternative to gelatin for vegetarians.*

Dulse: *Also known as "dillisk," it has a reddish-brown tint and is found on all the coasts of Ireland. It is often eaten dried, chewed like tobacco, or added to soups and stews. It needs to be cooked for a long time.*

Sloke: *Cooked sloke is just like spinach – hence its alternative name, sea spinach. It, too, is found on rocks all around Ireland's craggy coasts, one of the chief features of which is the awe-inspiring Giant's Causeway in County Antrim* (RIGHT)*.*

Sloke

▲ Wash well to remove all sand and grit. Soak for a few hours or overnight. Put in a pan with a little water and some butter. Cook very slowly for at least 4 hours. Serve with some lemon juice and young roast lamb.

Dulse

▲ Add dulse to fish or vegetable stews. Cook as follows: Wash the dulse to remove any bits of sand or grit. Cook in broth or water for 2-3 hours, then add to the soup or stew.

▲ If you want to serve it as a vegetable, strain it after cooking, put it back in the pan and cover with melted butter and black pepper.

Carrageen

COOKING TIME: 30 MINUTES + SETTING TIME

INGREDIENTS

$^1/_2$-1 tbsp carrageen

2$^1/_2$ cups milk

Grated zest of 1 lemon

Salt

1 tbsp sugar

Whipped cream

▲ Cover the dried carrageen with cold water, and soak for 15 minutes. Place in a saucepan with the milk, lemon zest and salt. Bring to a boil and simmer until it coats the back of a spoon.

▲ Add the sugar and stir until dissolved. Strain into a wet mold and leave in the refrigerator to set. Turn onto a pretty dish, pipe with cream and serve with fruit.

Seaweed Salad

PREPARATION AND COOKING TIME:
ABOUT 20 MINUTES

INGREDIENTS

A handful of egg noodles
Small piece of fresh root ginger
3 garlic cloves
1 bunch of scallions
1 leek
1 Romaine lettuce
Watercress
Handful of soaked seaweed
Soy sauce and oyster sauce
Sesame seeds, toasted

▲ Cook the egg noodles, drain well and keep to one side.
▲ Shred all the vegetables, watercress and seaweed, then stir fry in a little oil for about 3 minutes. Add 1 tbsp each of soy sauce and oyster sauce.
▲ Cook for another 2 minutes, then mix with the noodles.
▲ Arrange on a pretty white dish and scatter the sesame seeds on top. This is good warm or cold.

Colcannon is always served on Halloween. I remember eating huge platefuls of it for lunch. On Halloween, a silver coin was wrapped in paper and dropped into the colcannon. We would eat copious amounts of it for lunch until the money was found. After that we rapidly lost interest! Nevertheless, it is a very satisfying winter dish. It is traditionally made with kale, but you may substitute green Savoy or curly cabbage.

Sorrel-Stuffed Turnips

COOKING TIME: 30 MINUTES

INGREDIENTS

6 medium-sized turnips

¼ cup butter

1½-2 lb sorrel

1¼ cups béchamel sauce
(see Basic Recipes)

Chopped fresh parsley

▲ Scrub the turnips and cook in boiling water until tender, about 20 minutes. Keep warm.

▲ Melt the butter in a pan and drop in the sorrel. It almost melts in the butter. Scoop out the middles of the turnips and chop into the sorrel.

▲ Pack the stuffing in the cavities of the turnips. Keep warm in the oven, mix a little parsley with the béchamel sauce, and pour some over each stuffed turnip.

Colcannon

COOKING TIME: ABOUT 20-25 MINUTES

INGREDIENTS

3 lb potatoes

¾ cup butter

Milk

1 bunch of scallions or chives,
finely chopped

1 lb kale or green cabbage, cooked and
finely chopped

Salt and pepper

Grated nutmeg

▲ Cook and mash the potatoes. Add the butter and milk and beat until well creamed.

▲ Then add the finely chopped scallions or chives and cooked kale or cabbage. Season well with the salt and pepper and nutmeg.

Boxty on the Griddle

INGREDIENTS

2 large potatoes
1 parsnip
1 onion
1 tsp baking powder
Salt and pepper
2 large eggs, beaten
A little mashed potato

▲ Peel and grate the potatoes and parsnip. Squeeze as much water as possible out of the potatoes. Finely chop the onion and add to the parsnip and potatoes. Then add all the other ingredients and mix well.
▲ Spoon the boxty onto a hot griddle or skillet and cook on both sides. Serve with bacon and eggs for breakfast, or with apple sauce for high tea. Traditional boxty does not have parsnip in the recipe, but it gives a very good flavor to the pancake.

Stuffed Onions

COOKING TIME: 2 HOURS

INGREDIENTS	FOR THE STUFFING:
6 large Spanish onions	2½ cups chopped ham
Knob of butter	2 cups fresh white bread crumbs
Bread crumbs and grated cheese	¼ lb bacon slices
Broth	1 tsp chopped fresh mixed sweet herbs
	1 tomato, skinned and chopped
	Béchamel sauce (see Basic Recipes)

OVEN TEMPERATURE: 375°-400°F

▲ Preheat the oven. Cut the roots from the onions and remove the outer thin layer of skin. Cook the onions in a large pot of boiling salted water on top of the oven for about 1 hour. Remove from the water with a slotted spoon. Test with a skewer: They should be cooked, but not falling apart.
▲ With a sharp pointed knife, cut a circle from the stem end of each onion. Then carefully remove the cores of the onions. Do not remove so much that it collapses. Chop the cores of the onions and mix with the stuffing ingredients and a little béchamel. Pack into the onions and mound the stuffing above the top of the onion into a dome shape.
▲ Place the onions in a baking dish with the butter. Sprinkle the tops with bread crumbs and a little grated cheese. Bake for about 1 hour. If they appear to dry during the cooking, baste them with a little broth. Serve very hot.

Salsify Fritters

COOKING TIME: 15 MINUTES

INGREDIENTS

2 lb salsify
Juice of ½ lemon, or 1 tbsp vinegar
and water
3-4 tbsp all purpose flour
2 eggs
Salt and pepper

▲ Scrape the earth, grit and black skins off the salsify. Cut into 1½-in pieces and steep in acidulated water until you are ready to cook.
▲ Make a thin batter with the flour, eggs, salt and pepper. Cook the plain chopped salsify in boiling salted water for 10 minutes, then drain and pat dry with paper towels. Dip in the batter and fry in hot oil. Drain on paper towels and serve hot.

Salsify Fritters

This is another traditional Irish potato dish. It is served in soup bowls in a mound with a well made in the middle for some melted butter.

Champ or Cally

Potato and Celery Root Purée

COOKING TIME: 20-30 MINUTES

INGREDIENTS

2 lb floury potatoes
1 celery root
¼ cup butter
A little milk
Salt and pepper

▲ Peel the potatoes and celery root. Cut into even-sized pieces and cook in salted water until tender. Drain and keep over a low heat for a few minutes to get rid of excess moisture.

▲ Mash very well with the butter and milk. Don't make it too sloppy. Season with salt and pepper. Brown a little under the broiler and serve with game or roast beef.

Champ or Cally

COOKING TIME: 20 MINUTES

INGREDIENTS

8 potatoes (new floury ones are best)
6 scallions
Good ¾ cup milk
Pepper and salt
Chopped fresh thyme
½ cup butter

▲ Boil the potatoes until tender. Drain well and put them back over a very low heat, covering the pan with a clean dishtowel to dry out the potatoes. Then mash the potatoes thoroughly.

▲ Chop the scallions finely, using both the green and white parts. Place them in the milk and bring to a boil. Then pour the milk and onions onto the mashed potato and mash them in. Do not make it too sloppy. If this happens, dry out a little over a low heat.

▲ Season, and add a little fresh thyme to the now creamy mash. Put in bowls with little wells of butter in the middle.

There are many versions of potato cakes in Ireland. Here are two.

Sweet-and-Sour Red Cabbage
COOKING TIME: 1 HOUR OR MORE

INGREDIENTS

1 onion, sliced

Butter

1 red cabbage, shredded

1 large cooking apple, sliced

Approx 2½ cups vegetable or meat broth

Juniper berries

Cloves

1 tbsp brown sugar

1 tbsp red wine or cider

▲ Soften the onion slices in butter. Add the shredded cabbage and cook for a few minutes. Stir in the sliced apple, broth, berries and cloves to taste, and the other ingredients.

▲ Simmer for at least 1 hour, and longer, if desired. Red cabbage is not spoiled by long cooking.

▲ Serve with any game or pork dishes or Irish stew.

Potato Cakes 1
COOKING TIME: 25 MINUTES

INGREDIENTS

6 tbsp butter

1½ cups self rising flour

Salt and pepper

1½ cups freshly mashed potato

A little milk

Butter

Bacon

OVEN TEMPERATURE: 425°F

▲ Preheat the oven. Cut the butter into the flour, with a pinch of salt and pepper. Mix with the mashed potato and enough milk to make a soft dough.

▲ Roll out onto a floured board and cut into circles or triangles. Place on a lightly oiled tray and bake for 25 minutes. Serve hot split with butter and bacon.

Potato Cakes 2
COOKING TIME: 20 MINUTES

INGREDIENTS

¼ cup butter

Scant 1 cup all purpose flour

½ tsp salt

½ tsp baking powder

3 cups freshly mashed potatoes

Butter

▲ Cut the butter into the flour. Add the salt and baking powder and mix well. Mix in the potatoes and knead for a few minutes.

▲ Roll out onto a well-floured board with a floured rolling pin. Cook on a dry griddle or skillet until brown on both sides. Serve hot, dripping with butter.

Mixed Vegetable Salad with
Irish Salad Dressing

PREPARATION TIME: 20 MINUTES

1 lb mixed vegetables, such as potatoes,
carrots, leeks, asparagus, peas
and beans

Scallions, finely chopped

Finely chopped radishes and fresh chives

1 hard-cooked egg, chopped

SALAD DRESSING:

2 hard-cooked egg yolks

1 tsp Dijon mustard or dry mustard

1 tbsp white-wine vinegar or lemon juice

⅔ cup light cream

Salt and pepper

▲ Cut the vegetables into cubes or julienne strips. Cook until they are just tender but still crisp. Refresh in cold water to prevent overcooking.

▲ Make the dressing: Pound the hard-cooked egg yolks with the mustard, then add the vinegar and mix to a paste. Add the cream in a thin stream. Season to taste and mix with the salad vegetables.

▲ Finally, sprinkle with the chopped scallions, radishes, chives and hard-cooked egg.

This salad is very good with smoked salmon and with any herring dishes. It is also delicious on its own, accompanied with soda bread for a light lunch.

Michaelmas Salad

PREPARATION TIME: 10 MINUTES

INGREDIENTS

1½ lb freshly boiled beets
Bunch of scallions
Bunch of chopped fresh dill
2 tbsp chopped fresh parsley
2 hard-cooked eggs, chopped
2 boiled potatoes, diced
Olive oil
1 garlic clove, crushed
Lemon juice

▲ Put the first six ingredients in a glass bowl. Dress with a vinaigrette made with the olive oil, garlic and lemon juice. As a general rule combine in the following proportions – ⅓ lemon juice to ⅔ olive oil – and add garlic to taste. Toss well and serve at once.

Desserts, Breads and Baking

LEFT

*Rich sheaves of wheat, golden in the Irish sun, await collection to be milled into
flour to create Ireland's cornucopia of cakes and breads.*

Whiskey Trifle

INGREDIENTS

2 jelly rolls, or 1 lb sponge cake

Unsweetened preserved fruit, or a mixture of chopped fresh soft fruits (peaches, pears, berries, bananas, apricots)

2/3 cup whiskey

1¼ cups heavy cream

3 egg whites

Chopped almonds

FOR THE CUSTARD:

1 egg

3 egg yolks

1 tbsp sugar

2½ cups milk

1 vanilla bean

▲ Cut the jelly rolls into slices and drench them with whiskey. Line the bottom and sides of a glass bowl or soufflé dish with the slices, then put a layer of fruit inside the sponge lining. Then make the custard.

▲ In a bowl, beat the egg and egg yolks together with the sugar. In a saucepan, scald the milk with the vanilla bean. Then strain the milk over the eggs and sugar, beating all the time.

▲ Cook the custard in the bowl over boiling water until it coats the back of a wooden spoon. Make sure the boiling water does not actually touch the bottom of the bowl, or you will end up with scrambled eggs.

▲ Pour the custard over the cake and fruit while hot. Leave to cool. Whip the cream and in another bowl whip the egg whites until stiff. Fold them into the whipped cream. Pile the white froth on top of the trifle and decorate with chopped walnuts.

A DROP OF THE HARD STUFF

It was Catholic monks who probably brought the art of distilling from the Continent to Ireland during the 5th and 6th centuries, but it was the Irish who developed and refined the skills of whiskey distillation. Today, the Bushmill's distilleries (TOP) are one of the only two now in operation, producing its own unique product (casked, above). The label (RIGHT) dates from the 1870s.

Irish Coffee Cake

PREPARATION AND COOKING TIME:
10 MINUTES + 40-50 MINUTES

INGREDIENTS

½ cup butter

½ cup superfine sugar

2 eggs

⅔ cup self-rising flour

2 tbsp black coffee

FOR THE SYRUP:

⅔ cup black coffee

¼ cup superfine sugar

1 tbsp Irish whiskey

DECORATION:

1¼ cups heavy cream

Glacé frosting with whiskey

OVEN TEMPERATURE: 325°F

▲ Preheat the oven. Cream the butter and sugar together until light and fluffy. Add the eggs, one at a time, adding a little of the flour after each egg. Beat in the coffee, then fold in the rest of the flour.

▲ Divide the mixture in half and place in two 8-in round cake pans and bake for about 40 minutes.

▲ To make the syrup, heat the coffee with the sugar until it melts, then add the whiskey. When the cake is almost cool, prick the underside with a fork and drip the syrup all over the cake. Fill the middle with whipped cream and whiskey.

▲ Make a glacé frosting by adding a few drops of coffee to some sifted confectioners' sugar, then beating with a wooden spoon until it becomes glossy and can spread easily with a palette knife. Spread the frosting on the top of the cake.

Pears in Red Wine

COOKING TIME: ABOUT 1 HOUR

INGREDIENTS
---

8 good-sized Comice pears
Lemon juice and water
½ bottle sweet red wine
4 tbsp sugar
1 vanilla bean
1 stick of cinnamon
1 tbsp cornstarch
Cream

▲ Peel the pears carefully and place in acidulated water. Put the wine, sugar, vanilla bean and cinnamon in a pan and heat until dissolved.
▲ Poach the pears in the liquid until they are almost transparent. Drain the pears, reserve the liquid and blend it with the cornstarch.
▲ Cook the syrup again for a few minutes until thickened, then pour it over the pears and chill. Serve with pouring cream.

Irish Coffee

INGREDIENTS
---

2 tbsp Irish whiskey
1 tsp brown sugar
⅔ cup strong coffee
TO SERVE:
3 tbsp heavy cream, lightly whipped

▲ Having warmed an Irish coffee, or long, glass, add the sugar and whiskey and pour on the coffee. It is important to use a strong brew, so that the coffee complements the whiskey, rather than being drowned by it.
▲ To serve, pour the cream over a spoon onto the coffee and drink the warm liquid through the cool layer of cream.

Irish Coffee, the perfect end to an
Irish meal.

INGREDIENTS

⅓ cup slivered almonds

⅔ cup rolled oats

1¼ cups heavy or whipping cream

4 tbsp honey, to taste

4 tbsp whiskey

1 tbsp lemon juice

Raspberries

Cranachan

PREPARATION TIME: 20 MINUTES

▲ Toast the almonds and oatmeal.

▲ Whip the cream in a bowl, and stir in the honey and whiskey. Fold in the almonds and oatmeal, and finally, the lemon juice. Serve in tall glasses, garnished with raspberries.

Chocolate and Almond Sandwich

·*PREPARATION AND COOKING TIME:*
20 MINUTES + COOLING

INGREDIENTS

½ cup butter
5 tbsp sugar
1 egg, beaten
6 tbsp all purpose flour
6 tbsp blanched almonds, ground
1 tbsp cocoa
1 tsp baking powder
¼ tsp salt
3 tbsp milk
Confectioners' sugar

CHOCOLATE FILLING:

4 squares semisweet chocolate, grated
1½ tbsp milk
1 cup confectioners' sugar
6 tbsp unsalted butter
Dash of almond extract
OVEN TEMPERATURE: 400°F

▲ Preheat the oven. Cream the butter and sugar together. Add the well-beaten egg.

▲ In another bowl, sift together the flour, ground almonds, cocoa, baking powder and salt. Add alternately with the milk to the creamed butter and sugar. Combine thoroughly.

▲ Divide the mixture between 2 greased baking pans and bake for 20 minutes. When cool, sandwich together with the chocolate filling and dredge the top of the cake with confectioners' sugar.

▲ To make the filling, mix the chocolate with the milk and warm over a low heat until the chocolate has melted. Remove from the heat, beat in the confectioners' sugar, then leave until cool.

▲ Cream the butter and then add the chocolate mixture and the almond extract; beat until light and creamy. Fill the chocolate sandwich.

> *The quantities are for eight tartlets. It is usually advisable to make more, as they are so delicious they have a very short, sweet life.*

Walnut and Caramel Tartlets

PREPARATION AND COOKING TIME: 30-40 MINUTES

INGREDIENTS

*½ lb sweet tart pastry dough
(see Basic Recipes)*

1 generous tbsp honey

⅔ cup heavy cream

1½ cups sugar

Pinch of cream of tartar

1½ cups walnut halves

OVEN TEMPERATURE: 400°F

▲ Preheat the oven. Make the dough and chill for about 30 minutes. Roll out the dough and line the tartlet molds and chill. Make sure the tartlet molds have a high edge. Bake blind until the edges of the dough begin to color and cool on a wine rack.

▲ To make the filling, mix together the honey and the cream in a bowl. Put the sugar, cream of tartar and ⅔ cup water in a deep, heavy-bottomed saucepan and heat until dissolved. Raise the heat and boil to a light amber caramel.

▲ Stir the cream mixture into the caramel – stand back from the pan as it spatters. Boil without stirring until it reaches the soft boil stage – 239°F on a candy thermometer. Be very careful handling this mixture, as it can cause severe burns.

▲ Turn the heat down and add the walnuts. Spoon the mixture into the tartlet shells and serve when cool.

INGREDIENTS

2½ cups milk and zest of 1 lemon
2 cups fresh bread crumbs
¼ cup unsalted butter
2 tbsp sugar
1 tbsp Madeira
2 egg yolks, beaten
Strawberry or raspberry jam
4 egg whites and heaped 1 cup sugar
Whipped cream

OVEN TEMPERATURE: 350°F
AND 275°F

Queen of Puddings

PREPARATION AND COOKING TIME:
15 + 45 MINUTES

▲ Preheat the oven to 350°F. Bring the milk to a boil on top of the stove with the lemon zest grated into it. Infuse for 5 minutes.

▲ Mix the bread crumbs, butter and 2 tbsp sugar in a bowl. Strain on the milk, add a little Madeira, and leave for 10 minutes. Then add beaten egg yolks.

▲ Pour the mixture into a baking dish and bake for about 20 minutes. Remove from the oven and spread the jam over the mixture.

▲ Whisk the egg whites until stiff and fold in the remaining sugar to make a meringue mixture. Place on top of the jam in the dish and make peaks, using a fork.

▲ Put in the oven at 325°F for 10 minutes. Then turn the oven down to 275°F or less for 15 minutes.

▲ Serve hot with whipped cream.

ABOVE *Tourists and local inhabitants sampling the brew straight from the still. The illicit still* (LEFT) *is concealed, it is hoped, from the eyes of the local police.*

THE MYSTIQUE OF POTEEN

*I*llicit whiskey – called in Gaelic "poteen" – has been part of the Irish tradition ever since government taxation in the early 17th century forced production out of the home and into hiding. It is the father of all other illegal whiskies, notably American 'moonshine', which grew out of the distilling skills introduced by Irish immigrants.

Being illegal, poteen had to be made secretly – a task that tested Irish ingenuity to its fullest. Stills were hidden in caves, secret rooms, hollow stacks of peat, remote sea coves and on the banks of quiet streams – in fact, anywhere the distillers thought their activities would go undetected. The basic equipment required is a kettle to heat the mash – traditionally, this was malted barley, though other ingredients are now often substituted – the worm through which the resulting vapor is passed and a barrel to cool the vapor back to liquid. This is "poteen," a strong, colorless spirit, with the raw kick of an unaged whiskey.

Curd cake is what is now known as cheesecake.

Saffron Cake

COOKING TIME: 45 MINUTES

INGREDIENTS

3 cups all purpose flour	⅔ cup raisins
4 tbsp sugar	½ cup candied peel
Good pinch of salt	1 oz fresh yeast
½ cup butter	⅔ cup warm milk
Pinch of ground mace	Pinch of saffron
½ tsp ground cardamom seeds	

OVEN TEMPERATURE: 325°F

▲ Preheat the oven. Sift the flour, sugar and salt, then cut in the butter. Mix in the mace, cardamom, raisins and the peel.

▲ Mix the yeast with the milk until it becomes frothy, then stir in the saffron. Leave for a few minutes and beat into the dry mixture.

▲ Mix with your hands and leave in a warm place until it doubles in size. Turn onto a floured board and knead. Put into a round 8-in pan and leave to rise again.

▲ Bake in a medium oven for 45 minutes. Leave to cool on a rack.

Curd Cake

COOKING TIME: 30-35 MINUTES

INGREDIENTS

½ lb sweet tart pastry dough (see Basic Recipes)	4 tbsp sugar
2 eggs, separated	4 tbsp unsalted butter
1 lb cottage cheese, pressed through a strainer	Juice and grated zest of 1 lemon

OVEN TEMPERATURE: 350°F

▲ Preheat the oven. Make the sweet tart pastry dough and chill.

▲ Beat the egg yolks and mix with the cottage cheese, sugar, softened butter, lemon juice and zest. Combine well. Then whisk the egg whites until stiff. Fold them into the cottage cheese mixture.

▲ Roll out the dough and line an 8-in tart pan with a removable bottom. Bake blind until the edge of the pastry begins to color, then fill the pastry shell and bake for 30-35 minutes.

▲ Serve warm with melted strawberry or raspberry jam brushed over the surface.

Apple and Oat Cake

COOKING TIME: 30 MINUTES

INGREDIENTS

1½ lb cooking apples, peeled and sliced
4 tbsp light brown sugar
1 tsp ground cinnamon
⅓ cup raisins

▲ Preheat the oven. Cook the apples, sugar and cinnamon in a saucepan until the apples form a pulp. Then add the raisins and cool.

▲ Melt the butter, sugar and honey in another saucepan. In a bowl, mix the rolled oats and lemon zest together, then pour into the honey mixture. Add the eggs and whiskey and mix well.

▲ Divide the oatmeal mixture into thirds. Put 1 layer of the oatmeal on the bottom of a cake pan. Cover with half the apple mixture. Top this with another layer of oatmeal. Then add the final apple layer, then finish off with the oatmeal.

▲ Bake for 30 minutes. Serve warm with cream.

FOR THE OATMEAL PASTRY:

½ cup unsalted butter
Heaped 1 tbsp brown sugar
2 tbsp clear honey
3 cups rolled oats
Grated zest of 1 lemon
2 eggs, beaten
1 glass whiskey

OVEN TEMPERATURE: 375°F

INGREDIENTS

2 oranges

6 eggs

½ cup sugar

2 cups blanched almonds, ground

1 tsp baking powder

Flour to dredge the pan

FOR THE ICING:

1 cup cottage cheese

½ cup confectioners' sugar

2 tbsp heavy cream

1 tbsp Grand Marnier, or Cointreau

OVEN TEMPERATURE: 375°F

Boiled Orange and Almond Cake with Cottage Cheese Frosting

COOKING TIME: 2 HOURS

▲ Preheat the oven. Boil the oranges in their skins in water on top of the stove until they are very soft – this takes about 1 hour. Drain thoroughly.

▲ Beat the eggs and add the sugar, almonds and baking powder. Purée the chopped oranges in a food processor and add to the mixture. Oil and flour a 9-in cake pan and pour in the mixture. Bake for about 1 hour. This is a very moist cake and may be served as a dessert, plain with cream, or with the cottage cheese frosting.

▲ To make the frosting, put all the ingredients into a mixer or food processor. Blend. When they are well creamed, spread on top of the cake.

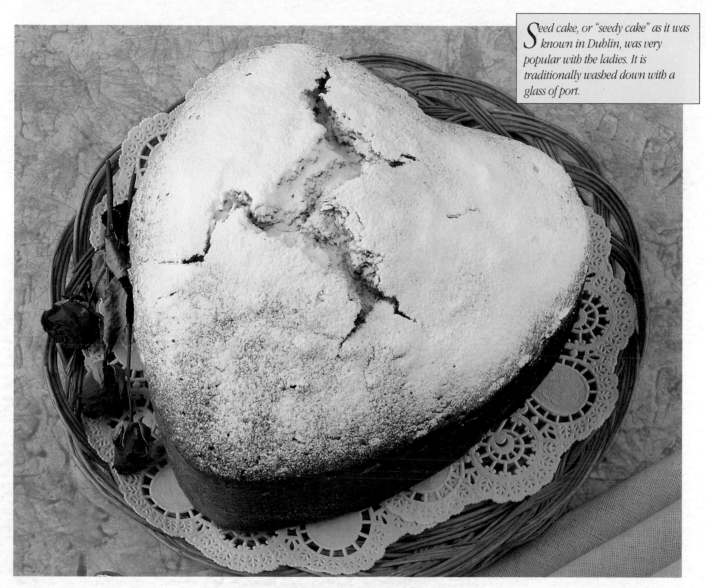

*S*eed cake, or "seedy cake" as it was known in Dublin, was very popular with the ladies. It is traditionally washed down with a glass of port.

Seed Cake

COOKING TIME: 1½ HOURS

▲ Cream the butter and sugar. Beat in the eggs, 1 at a time, adding a little flour each time to prevent the mixture curdling.

▲ Fold in the rest of the flour and the caraway seeds. Stir in the milk and kirsch.

▲ Bake in a round 8-in pan, lined and greased, for about 1½ hours. Leave in the pan for a few minutes, then cool on a wire rack. Dredge the top of the cake with confectioners' sugar, if wished. This cake keeps for a long time in an airtight container.

INGREDIENTS

1 cup butter

Heaped 1 cup sugar

4 eggs

1½ cups self-rising flour

1 heaped tbsp caraway seeds

2 tbsp milk

2 tbsp Kirsch

Confectioners' sugar

OVEN TEMPERATURE: 325°F

This recipe is from Marlfield House Restaurant in Co. Wexford.

ABOVE *Wexford has long been known as a center of culinary excellence; the recipe for Chocolate and Whiskey Cake here comes from one of its best-known restaurants.*

Chocolate and Whiskey Cake

PREPARATION TIME:
MINIMUM 4 HOURS, OR OVERNIGHT

INGREDIENTS

½ lb graham crackers

8 squares unsweetened cooking chocolate

1 cup butter

2 eggs

6 tbsp sugar

½ cup candied cherries

½ cup walnuts

⅔ cup Irish whiskey

⅓ cup heavy cream, whipped

▲ Crush the biscuits coarsely and keep them aside.

▲ Melt the chocolate with the butter in a double boiler or saucepan. Cream the eggs and sugar in a bowl until they are pale and thickened, then fold in the chocolate.

▲ To this mixture add three-quarters of the cherries and the walnuts; save the rest for decoration. Fold in all but 1 tbsp of whiskey.

▲ Oil a 9-in baking dish, line with the crushed biscuits, then scrape all of the mixture into it. Decorate the top with the remaining cherries and walnuts and place in the refrigerator for several hours or overnight. Take it out of the refrigerator about 30 minutes before serving.

▲ Add the whiskey to the cream. Pipe around the top of the cake.

This recipe is from Monica Sheridan's column in the Irish Times. *She inherited it from her mother and I have been making it for years with great success.*
When it was first published in the Irish Times, *Monica received letters from all over the world. There is a street in Rome where all the inhabitants make it every Christmas.*

INGREDIENTS

¾ cup candied cherries
2 cups seedless raisins
2 cups golden raisins
1 cup candied peel
½ cup chopped angelica
1½ cups chopped walnuts
1½ cups butter
1¾ cups sugar
7 eggs
2½ cups all purpose flour
1 tsp salt
1 tsp apple pie spice
Irish whiskey

OVEN TEMPERATURE: BETWEEN 300°F
AND 275°F

Christmas Cake

PREPARATION AND COOKING TIME:
SEVERAL HOURS OR 1 DAY + 6 HOURS

▲ Some hours (or a day) before making the cake, the following preparations are necessary. Preheat the oven to 275°F. Halve the cherries and put, together with the rest of the fruit and nuts, into a casserole. Mix them well together. Cover loosely with paper or foil and put into the warm oven until the fruit is well heated through.

▲ Toss the fruit and nuts once or twice to allow the heat to penetrate. This heating makes the fruit sticky and prevents it from sinking to the bottom of the cake. It also makes it plump and juicy. When all the fruit is heated through, take it out of the oven and let it go cold.

▲ Cream the butter and sugar together until white and fluffy. Add the eggs, 1 at a time, with 1 tsp of flour for each egg. This prevents the mixture from curdling.

▲ Sift the remaining flour with the salt and apple pie spice. Fold into the egg mixture, then fold in the fruit and nuts.

▲ Put the mixture into a deep 10-in greased cake pan that has been well lined with two thicknesses of wax paper. Flatten the mixture in the pan and make sure there is about 2 in of the pan above the mixture.

▲ Trim the lining paper level with the top of the pan and rest an inverted heatproof plate or lid over it.

▲ Put the cake in a low (300°F) oven for 1 hour, then reduce the heat to 275°F for another 5 hours. The cake should be golden when ready. Do not remove it from the pan until it is cold. Then prick the bottom with a skewer and sprinkle liberally with Irish whiskey. This cake keeps for a long time in an airtight container.

Brown Soda Bread

PREPARATION AND COOKING TIME:
ABOUT 15 MINUTES + 40 MINUTES

INGREDIENTS

6 cups whole-wheat flour

3 cups hard white flour

1 heaped tsp baking soda

13 heaped tsp baking powder

2 eggs

*Approx 2½ cups plain yogurt mixed
with the water to the consistency
of buttermilk*

Good pinch of salt

*OVEN TEMPERATURE: 375°F, REDUCED
TO 350°F*

▲ Preheat the oven. Place all the dry ingredients in a large mixing bowl.
Combine well with the fingers.

▲ In another bowl mix the eggs with the yogurt and water.

▲ Make a well in the dry mixture and slowly pour on the yogurt and
water. Mix with your hands until you get a nice soft dough – not too wet.
A dough that is too wet or too stiff will result in a hard and heavy bread.

▲ Lightly flour a worktop or pastry board. Divide the dough in half. Make
2 flat rounds of bread on the board.

▲ Cut a deep cross in the middle of each loaf. Place in the preheated
oven for 10 minutes, then reduce the heat. Bake until the bottom of the
bread sounds hollow when knocked. This takes about 30 minutes.

*I*rish soda bread is arguably the best
bread in the world.
*Many women in Ireland still make it
every day. There is no waiting for it to
rise, nor does it involve endless
kneading. The less soda bread is
handled the better it will be. The
following quantities will make two
1½ lb loaves. I have substituted
yogurt and water for the traditionally
used buttermilk.*

Irish Soda Bread

INGREDIENTS

4 cups all purpose flour

1 tsp salt

2 tsp baking soda

1½ tsp cream of tartar

2 tbsp lard

1¼ cups buttermilk

OVEN TEMPERATURE: 425°F

MAKES 1 LOAF

▲ Sift the flour, salt, baking soda and cream of tartar into a bowl. Rub in the lard and add enough buttermilk to make a soft dough. Turn the mixture on to a lightly floured board and knead for a minute. Shape into a round and place on the baking sheet. Mark with a cross, cutting deep into the dough.

▲ Bake for 40-50 minutes, until lightly browned and firm when tapped on the base. Cool the bread on a wire rack.

VARIATIONS: You can use plain milk instead of buttermilk, but if you do, double the quantity of cream of tartar.

Oatcakes

COOKING TIME: ABOUT 20 MINUTES

INGREDIENTS

½ cup medium rolled oats

Pinch of salt

Pinch of baking soda

1 tbsp melted bacon fat

Hot water

All purpose flour

▲ Mix the dry ingredients in a bowl, make a well in the center and pour in the melted fat. Add enough hot water to make a stiff paste.

▲ Scatter your work surface or board liberally with rolled oats and transfer the paste to the board, pressing with the hands. (Cover your hands with flour as the oatmeal is very sticky at this stage.)

▲ Roll to about ¼ in thickness and cut into 8-in circles. Sprinkle with more rolled oats, then cut into quarters.

▲ Place on a hot griddle – a heavy skillet will do – and cook until the edges curl a little. Then turn them over and cook on the other side, or finish them under a warm broiler.

▲ They may also be baked in a medium oven (350°F) for about 20 minutes.

This is another of Monica Sheridan's recipes.

Irish Coffee Pudding

PREPARATION TIME: ABOUT 1 HOUR

INGREDIENTS

6 eggs, separated

Heaped 1 cup sugar

1¼ cups very strong black coffee

1½ oz leaf gelatin

1¼ cups heavy cream

7 tbsp Irish whiskey

Whiskey-flavored whipped cream (optional)

6 tbsp crushed walnuts (optional)

▲ In a bowl, cream the egg yolks with the sugar. Heat the coffee and dissolve the gelatin in it, then add it to the yolks and the sugar. Beat well.

▲ Put the bowl over a pan of boiling water and heat, stirring, until the mixture begins to thicken. Remove from the heat and, when the bowl has cooled a little, put it over cracked ice and continue to stir.

▲ When the mixture is on the point of setting, whip the cream and fold it in, together with the whiskey. Then fold in the stiffly beaten egg whites.

▲ Pour into individual glasses and leave to set. If desired, top with whiskey-flavored whipped cream and crushed walnuts.

I nstead of pastry, potato-cake dough is used for the crust. It is always baked on the top of the stove on a griddle or in a heavy iron pan. This is Monica Sheridan's version.

Potato and Apple Cake

COOKING TIME: ABOUT 30 MINUTES

INGREDIENTS

FOR THE POTATO CAKE MIXTURE:

4 tbsp butter
¾ cup all purpose flour
½ tsp salt
½ tsp baking powder
1 lb freshly washed potatoes

FOR THE APPLE MIXTURE:

2 large cooking apples
A little sugar to taste
4-5 cloves
1 tsp cinnamon
2 tbsp butter

▲ Make a portion of potato-cake mixture (*see* Potato Cakes 2 for method). Divide the dough in two parts and roll out into two circles.
▲ Peel the apples and slice thinly. Put a few layers of them on one circle of dough. Cover with the other circle of dough and pinch the edges together. Cook gently on a greased pan, turning once to cook on the other side.
▲ When the apples are cooked through, lift back the top and sprinkle with sugar, cloves and cinnamon. Add a large pat of butter.
▲ Replace the top, leave on the heat for another 5 minutes, and eat very hot with cream or egg custard.

This version of brack – fruit bread – is made with baking powder, cold tea and Irish whiskey.

Irish Tea Brack

DESSERTS, BREADS AND BAKING

Barm Brack

PREPARATION AND COOKING TIME:
1 ½ + 1 HOUR

INGREDIENTS

Heaped 3 cups all purpose flour
Grated nutmeg
Pinch of salt
¼ cup butter
¾ oz yeast
2 tbsp sugar
1¼ cups milk
2 eggs, beaten
1½ cups golden raisins
1½ cups currants
1 cup candied peel

OVEN TEMPERATURE: 400°F

▲ Preheat the oven. Sift the flour, nutmeg and salt together. Cut the butter into the flour.
▲ Cream the yeast in a cup with 1 tsp of the sugar. Add the rest of the sugar to the flour mixture and combine well. Scald the milk; add to the liquid yeast together with all but a little of the well-beaten eggs. Stir into the dry ingredients to produce a stiff but elastic batter. Fold in the fruit.
▲ Butter an 8-in round cake pan and pour in the dough. It should come halfway up the pan. Cover with a clean cloth and leave in a warm place to rise – it should double in size in about 1 hour.
▲ Brush the top of the brack with beaten egg to glaze. Bake until a skewer, or thin knife, comes out clean – about 1 hour.

Irish Tea Brack

PREPARATION TIME:
OVERNIGHT + 1 HOUR COOKING

INGREDIENTS

1 lb golden raisins
1 lb raisins
2½ cups brown sugar
2 cups black tea
2 cups Irish whiskey
Heaped 3 cups all purpose flour
3 eggs, beaten
1 tbsp baking powder
2 tsp apple pie spice

OVEN TEMPERATURE: 375°

▲ Soak the fruit with the sugar in the tea and whiskey overnight.
▲ Preheat the oven.
▲ Add the flour, eggs, baking powder and spices to the fruit mixture.
▲ Mix all the ingredients together well and put in greased bread pans.
▲ Bake for 1 hour. Allow to cool in the pan slightly before turning out to cool fully on a rack.

Guinness Cake

PREPARATION AND COOKING TIME:
OVERNIGHT + 2 HOURS

INGREDIENTS

½ cup butter
1 cup brown sugar
3 eggs, beaten
2¼ cups self-rising flour
½ tsp apple pie spice
Pinch of salt

⅔ cup raisins, soaked in Guinness overnight
½ cup candied peel, soaked
1⅓ cups golden raisins, soaked
¼ cup candied cherries
⅔ cup Guinness or dark beer

OVEN TEMPERATURE: 350°F

▲ Preheat the oven. Cream the butter and sugar until the sugar is dissolved. Beat in the eggs.
▲ Add the flour, salt, apple pie spice and the soaked dried fruit.
▲ Finally mix in the Guinness.
▲ Grease a deep 8-in cake pan and pour the mixture in. Bake for about 2 hours until firm in the center.

Apple and Elderberry Tart

COOKING TIME: 30 MINUTES

INGREDIENTS

½ lb sweet tart pastry dough
(see Basic Recipes)
2 lb tart eating apples
1¼ cups elderberries or other soft berries
Red currant jelly

OVEN TEMPERATURE: 400°F

▲ Preheat the oven. Make the dough, chill, then roll out and line a 10-in tart pan.
▲ Core and cut the apples into eighths. Place them in the tart pan in concentric circles. Scatter the elderberries on top of the apples. Melt the red currant jelly and spread on top of the tart. Bake until the pastry is a golden brown. Serve with cream or with egg custard.

Basic Recipes

LEFT
*The Four Courts in Dublin, once
a hated symbol of the British
Ascendancy, but now restored to
their former 18th-century glory.*

Broths

There is no such thing as a good soup without a good broth. Like anything else in the Irish cooking tradition, broths are extremely simple to make – it just takes a little care and decent ingredients. There are four basic types of broth which may be used for soups and casseroles. Broths may also be reduced and frozen – a little broth-making session now and again can transform your cooking. Remember, nothing good ever comes out of a commercial bouillon cube.

White or Poultry Broth

COOKING TIME: 2 HOURS

INGREDIENTS

1 boiling fowl or poultry carcass
(pork or veal bones may be used also)

2 large onions

1 leek

2 carrots

4 garlic cloves

4 stalks and leaves of celery

1 large bunch of mixed fresh herbs –
thyme, parsley, oregano and sage

1 bay leaf

▲ Put the chicken or bones in a large pot. Clean and peel all the vegetables but leave them whole and add, together with 6½ pt water, to the pot. Tie the herbs together and put it in the pot. Bring slowly to a boil, then simmer for 2 hours.

▲ Skim any scum or froth off the top; strain the liquid off the vegetables as they will make the stock cloudy if they are left in. Leave in a cold place and take any oil or fat off the top.

▲ You now have a lovely clear stock, which may be reduced and concentrated by boiling very fast and frozen for future use.

Brown Broth

COOKING TIME: 1 HOUR 30 MINUTES

▲ Use beef, veal, lamb, ham or pork bones, or any combination of these. Ask your butcher or meat counter attendant to break up the bones. Clean and prepare the same vegetables as for white or poultry stock, with the addition of some white turnips.

▲ Put the bones in a hot oven to brown, basting now and again. After about 30 minutes, take them out, drain off any fat and put them in a large saucepan. Brown the vegetables in the fat and add them to the bones.

▲ Cover with 6½ pt water and add the bunch of herbs and continue as for the white stock.

Vegetable Broth

COOKING TIME: 30 MINUTES

INGREDIENTS

2 lb potato peelings

2 tbsp olive oil

2 large onions, coarsely chopped

10 garlic cloves

1 leek, chopped

2 celery stalks, chopped

2 carrots, coarsely chopped

2 turnips, coarsely chopped

A few fresh or dried mushrooms

4 soft tomatoes

Large bunch of herbs

There is no need for vegetarian soups to be insipid, watery affairs. A potato-peel broth gives a good base to any vegetable soup or stew.
NOTE: *You will notice that I have not added salt or pepper to the broths. Adding salt is dangerous, as the broth may be greatly reduced and become too salty to use – it is better to wait and season the final dish.*

▲ Scrub and peel the potatoes. Put only the peelings in a large pot with the olive oil – add all the other coarsely chopped vegetables. Brown them a little, then add 3¾ pt water and the herbs and simmer for 30 minutes.

▲ Strain and use for soups, sauces and stews.

Fish Broth

COOKING TIME: 20 MINUTES

*Fish broth is so quick to make that it is not really worth bothering to freeze it.
Use any white fish bones and heads – avoid oily fish because it becomes too strong and has a rather unpleasant taste, reminiscent of cod liver oil.
Salmon may be used for salmon dishes but otherwise this is also too oily.*

INGREDIENTS

¼ cup unsalted butter

2 onions, sliced

1 lb fish heads, trimmings and bones

4 garlic cloves

1 head of fennel, sliced (optional)

Bunch of parsley, chopped

2 bay leaves, torn

1 piece of lemon peel

Lemon juice

5 cups mixed white wine and water

▲ Soften the onions in a little unsalted butter. Add the other ingredients and cover with the water and the wine. Simmer for about 20 minutes. Strain and cool.

▲ A shellfish broth may be made with shellfish trimmings or shells and a few mussels.

ABOVE AND RIGHT *Cows being
driven home from the fields for
evening milking, and grazing
peacefully in rich pasture – a
traditional Irish scene that has
barely changed over the centuries.*

Piecrust Pastry Dough

PREPARATION TIME:
10 MINUTES + 30 MINUTES

INGREDIENTS
1⅓ cups all purpose flour
Pinch of salt
½ cup unsalted butter
1 egg yolk
OVEN TEMPERATURE: 400°F

▲ Put the flour and salt in a bowl. Cut the butter into small pieces and cut into the flour until the mixture resembles bread crumbs.
▲ Make a well in the center and add the egg yolk, then mix in some iced water – enough to make a firm dough.
▲ Rest the mixture in the refrigerator for about 30 minutes, then use as required.
▲ Bake at 400°F until golden.

Sweet Tart Pastry Dough

INGREDIENTS
1⅓ cups all purpose flour
5 tbsp sugar
Pinch of salt
6 tbsp unsalted butter
3 egg yolks
Vanilla to taste

▲ Mix all the dry ingredients together. Chop the butter and blend into the flour mixture until it looks like fine bread crumbs.
▲ Mix in the egg yolks and vanilla until you have a firm dough. Chill for 30 minutes before rolling out.

Flaky or Puff Pastry Dough

PREPARATION TIME: 1 HOUR

INGREDIENTS
2¼ cups all purpose flour
Good pinch of salt
1 cup unsalted butter, cut into
small pieces

▲ Sift the flour and salt into a large bowl. Cut in ½ cup of the butter, then add ⅔ cup ice-cool water and combine to form a stiff mixture. Rest for about 20 minutes in the refrigerator.
▲ Roll out the dough and spread the rest of the butter over one third. Fold the dough over to cover the butter and roll out again gently, making sure the butter does not come through the dough. If this happens you will have a very oily rather than a crisp, flaky pastry.
▲ Fold the dough into thirds. Rest it for 5 minutes and roll out again. Finally, roll the dough out until ⅛ in thick and use for sweet or savory pies.
▲ When ready to use, cook at 400°F until well-risen and golden brown.

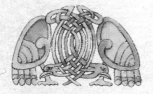

Béchamel Sauce

COOKING TIME: 45 MINUTES
TO MAKE 2½ CUPS OF SAUCE

INGREDIENTS

2 tbsp unsalted butter
4 tbsp all purpose flour
2½ cups milk
2 bay leaves
Sprig of fresh thyme
1 onion
Freshly grated nutmeg
Salt and pepper to taste

▲ Prepare a roux: Melt the butter in a pan and mix in the flour over a low heat. Allow the roux to cook but not brown. Gradually add the milk, stirring or whisking continuously to prevent lumps forming.
▲ Bring the sauce to a boil, stirring. Add the herbs and onion and simmer for at least 30 minutes. Take care that the sauce does not burn or stick to the pan.
▲ When the sauce is ready, strain it and add the freshly grated nutmeg and seasoning.

VARIATIONS: Add some well-flavored, hard, grated cheese to taste for a rich cheese sauce. For a parsley sauce, add a handful of chopped fresh parsley and a little softened onion.

Tomato Sauce

COOKING TIME: 1 HOUR
TO MAKE 2½ CUPS OF SAUCE

INGREDIENTS

¼ cup olive oil or bacon fat
2 large onions, chopped
6 large garlic cloves, crushed
2 lb ripe tomatoes, peeled, seeded and chopped, or 2 × 14-oz can chopped tomatoes
Fresh parsley, thyme and bay leaves tied together
Salt and freshly ground black pepper
1 tbsp tomato paste
1 tbsp chopped fresh basil, if available, or parsley

▲ Heat the oil or fat in a pan and cook the onions and garlic for about 15 minutes. Add the tomatoes, herbs and seasoning and bring to a boil.
▲ Add the tomato paste, stir well and simmer for 45 minutes. Remove the pan from the heat, adjust the seasoning and add some chopped fresh basil, if in season, or parsley.

Hollandaise Sauce

MAKES 1⅓ CUPS OF SAUCE

INGREDIENTS

¾ cup unsalted butter
3 egg yolks
Salt
Juice of ½ lemon

▲ Melt the butter and let it cool a little. Remove any white scum from the surface.
▲ In a small, heavy-bottomed saucepan, beat the egg yolks with 3 tbsp water. Over a very low heat beat until the mixture is thick and creamy: On no account let the mixture get too hot.
▲ Take the pan off the heat and beat in the butter, drop by drop. When it begins to thicken add the butter a little faster. Add the salt and lemon juice to taste.

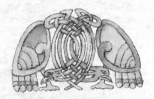

Green Mayonnaise

PREPARATION TIME: ABOUT 15 MINUTES

INGREDIENTS

2 egg yolks
Lemon juice
2½ cups sunflower oil
1 tbsp mixed chopped fresh herbs (basil, parsley, sorrel, cilantro, chives)
1 garlic clove
Salt

▲ Place the egg yolks in a mixer or blender or food processor with some lemon juice. Set the machine at a medium speed and at first gently drip the oil in. When it begins to emulsify, pour in a steady stream until the oil is used up.
▲ Pound the herbs with the garlic and salt in a mortar and pestle, then mix these in with the mayonnaise.
▲ This mayonnaise may be kept in a sealed container in the refrigerator.

Index